"Scott Boren is a sage of small group life and leadership. He w[illegible]s a veteran practitioner from down in the trenches. Scott leads us beyond the techniques of leading a good meeting—he calls us to embrace the richness that can only come when we follow in the way of Jesus."

Lance Witt, author of *Replenish*

"This is a game-changer! In this breakthrough message, Scott Boren gets beneath the surface of our superficial assumptions about small groups to uncover the life-giving way of the Master. I highly recommend this book to all pastors, leaders and followers of Christ!"

Andrew S. Mason, founder of smallgroupchurches.com

"Scott Boren writes in a winsome way and leads us to the core values behind effective small group leadership. . . . Offers time-tested principles that will help us become better small group leaders. I appreciated how Boren often illustrated a concept with a real life example rather than only explaining it. I will recommend this book to the leaders and pastors I'm coaching."

Joel Comiskey, president of Joel Comiskey Group

"Scott Boren, one of the most experienced leaders in the field of small groups and missional community, has given us a fresh perspective on how to experience life in and beyond group meetings. Rather than giving us a formula, Scott lays out proven principles that are scalable to multiple settings and scenarios of group life. Every group leader should read this book."

Tim Catchim, church planter and author of *The Permanent Revolution*

"When Scott talks, I listen. He combines missional fervor, a disciple-making focus and community-building passion here, calling us to something greater every time we gather in community."

Bill Donahue, author of *Leading Life-Changing Small Groups*

"Every pastor longs for renewal in small group ministry. In his *Leading Small Groups in the Way of Jesus,* Scott Boren provides the biblical foundation and theological imagination for such a renewal. Boren shows us the way to open up spaces for the presence of Christ among us, and then calls them 'small groups.'"

David Fitch, Northern Seminary, author of *Prodigal Christianity*

"This book was like a second salvation for me when it comes to leading and loving people the way Jesus did. When it comes to discipleship and biblical community, Scott Boren soars way past thought provoking—this book is one hundred percent kingdom provoking."

Scott Hagan, senior pastor of Real Life Church, Sacramento

LEADING SMALL GROUPS IN THE WAY OF JESUS

M. SCOTT BOREN

An imprint of InterVarsity Press
Downers Grove, Illinois

InterVarsity Press
P.O. Box 1400, Downers Grove, IL 60515-1426
ivpress.com
email@ivpress.com

InterVarsity Press® is the book-publishing division of InterVarsity Christian Fellowship/USA®, a movement of students and faculty active on campus at hundreds of universities, colleges and schools of nursing in the United States of America, and a member movement of the International Fellowship of Evangelical Students. For information about local and regional activities, visit intervarsity.org.

While any stories in this book are true, some names and identifying information may have been changed to protect the privacy of individuals.

Cover design: Cindy Kiple
Interior design: Beth McGill
Images: Empty map: © Teekid/iStockphoto
Brush stroke: © Peterfactors/iStockphoto
Pirate map: © FlamingPumpkin/iStockphoto

ISBN 978-0-8308-3681-9 (print)
ISBN 978-0-8308-9677-6 (digital)

Printed in the United States of America ♾

As a member of the Green Press Initiative, InterVarsity Press is committed to protecting the environment and to the responsible use of natural resources. To learn more, visit greenpressinitiative.org.

Library of Congress Cataloging-in-Publication Data
Boren, M. Scott
Leading small groups in the way of Jesus : / M. Scott Boren.
pages cm
Includes bibliographical references.
ISBN 978-0-8308-3681-9 (pbk. : alk. paper)
1. Church group work. 2. Small groups—Religious aspects—Christianity. I. Title.
BV652.2.B668 2015
253'.7--dc23

2014034474

P	20	19	18	17	16	15	14	13	12	11	10	9	8	7	6	5	4	3	2	1
Y	32	31	30	29	28	27	26	25	24	23	22	21	20	19	18	17	16	15		

To my mom and dad,

Gaylan and Grady Boren, the leaders of my first small group.

Thank you for leading me in the way of Jesus.

Contents

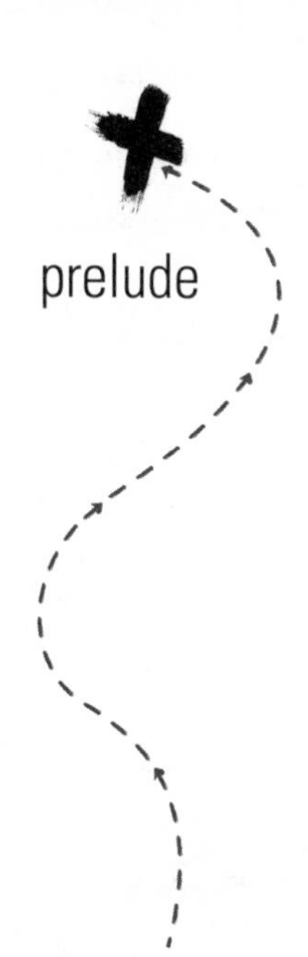

From Good Small Group Meetings to Great Group Experiences

For about a quarter of a century, I have been wrestling with leadership questions related to the church, small groups and midsized groups that are often called "missional communities." While in my early twenties I had the privilege of working for a training and consulting ministry that helped churches establish groups. Before groups became a popular trend in church circles, we were experimenting with new structures and strategies for living in community. As a result I've been able to work with almost every stream of church life conceivable, from those in the high-church Anglican tradition to nondenominational charismatics and all kinds in between.

Questions about group leadership cut across traditional boundaries. While the strategic emphasis on small groups is relatively new, the groups themselves are as old as time. For instance, as I reflect on my journey in the church I find that small groups have always been foundational; we just did not think about them in strategic ways. Even though the church of my childhood, Foote Baptist Church in rural North Texas, was made up of fewer than seventy people, small groups were part of our weekly experience. We called it Sunday school. We also had home Bible studies, leadership teams, committees and something called "cottage prayer meetings." Here's a list of the kinds of groups that I've experienced through the years:

- home groups
- task groups
- mission groups
- missional communities
- cell groups
- choir groups
- Bible study groups
- worship groups
- fellowship groups
- care groups
- recovery groups
- service project groups
- outreach groups
- leadership development groups
- church leadership groups
- committee groups
- short-term sermon study groups
- sports groups
- Sunday school groups

It's only natural that churches would get things done in groups since they're part of the warp and woof of how good living works. The small group form is one of those fundamental things in life that cannot be surpassed by some new innovation. There are certain basic things that have always been great, and no matter how smart we become, we can't come up with something better. These include the wheel for moving stuff, the three-legged stool (or tripod) for holding stuff up, a spherical ball for play and the small group for organizing life. We can invent better wheels, but we cannot invent something better than the wheel.

Likewise, we cannot improve on the small group as a fundamental form around which church life operates.

At the same time, not all groups are created equal. While groups were a natural part of the church of my childhood and early adulthood, they were left unexamined. For instance, at one point in my journey I was involved in seven different church groups at the same time. I was what you might call a Christian go-getter, and group involvement demonstrated my Christian devotion. While I had lots of surface conversations about Christian ideas and I did various tasks with lots of different people, something was lacking. And because we did not have a clear understanding of group dynamics and how to lead community, my involvement in all of these groups was applauded.

We were doing groups—and many today are doing the same thing—but we were not looking at what they were producing. Group involvement. Group growth. Group reproduction. All of this was happening then. And it happens now. But it's not enough. We must examine what we are generating through all of this group activity.

One night about fifteen years ago, I left work to head to my small group. At the time I was coaching group leaders in the church, but this was the group in which I participated as a member. On the way I stopped for dinner, and while eating my calzone I realized I did not want to go. I felt guilty. I had been a small group staff pastor, I had led training seminars across the country on leading groups, and I was then the editor of a magazine for small group leaders. I was supposed to be committed to a group. I taught people how we needed one another. I wrote about God's commands for us to love one another. However, that night I paid attention to something deep within me. I allowed myself to be honest. I ordered some baklava and went home.

Now skipping a group gathering for the sake of enjoying baklava might not seem like a big deal, but I'm the type of person who tends to do things out of a sense of duty and obligation. I was raised to go to meetings—especially church meetings—whether I wanted to or not. But this moment of honesty set me on a new path. It opened up space for me to look beneath all the activities so I could see what kind of life our groups were producing.

In this situation, the source of my angst was not the leader. I liked the couple that led the group. I enjoyed the people in the group. And I believed in the vision of the church. In addition, the group meetings were pretty good. We had good curriculum and meaningful discussions, and we were open for others to join us.

However, we had a disease. We suffered from what I've come to call "good meeting syndrome." We were good for two hours on Thursday night, but our group didn't have any life beyond that. People attended every week, but we fell short of experiencing anything more than Bible discussions, a few worship songs and some cookies. For many of us, a good weekly meeting was better than no meeting at all. But we had a vision for much more—a vision for loving one another, for making a difference in the world and for growing as disciples. And our good group meeting was not producing what we had hoped to experience.

As I work with churches, I find that many (if not most) groups suffer from good meeting syndrome: they're good but not great. This applies to both leading small groups of five to fifteen people to midsize gatherings ("missional communities") of twenty to fifty. In fact, when we're honest, many of us will admit that we're not looking for meetings at all. We might say we want a Bible study or a weekly meeting to attend, but in the deep places of our hearts we're looking to find others with whom we can be our authentic selves. We long to love and be loved. We don't often say it, but what we want is to find some people for whom we don't have to perform to be accepted.

Leading good group meetings might be enough to carry a group forward in the early stages of its development, but it won't be what causes a group to flourish and move into greatness. It won't be the thing that causes people to want to give up their baklava and a quiet evening at home. Good group meetings serve as doors to more—something Jesus describes after he washed the feet of the disciples: "A new command I give you: Love one another. As I have loved you, so you must love one another. By this everyone will know that you are my disciples, if you love one another" (John 13:34-35).

These words came at the end of a small group meeting led by Jesus—one that included washing feet, sharing a meal, Judas leaving with intentions of betrayal and predictions that Peter would deny Jesus. This was more than a good meeting. In fact, by our standards today, it might fall short of a *good* group gathering. This was not a nice Bible study followed by prayer requests and cookies. It was messy. It was honest. It ended with more questions than answers. But it was *great.*

This group experience was more than a discussion about the ways of Jesus. It was a demonstration of the way Jesus wanted them to live. Jesus led his small group in the way of Jesus.

Sally's story illustrates this shift. Sally had been told by her pastor that leading group members beyond a good meeting mentality meant people had to open up about their lives. They had to be transparent. So she led the way, moving beyond offering ideas and giving "right" answers to sharing how she fell short or struggled with the topic the group was discussing. But after six months of being the only one to do this, she was ready to give up and return to the old way. At that point she decided to give it one more shot.

Jeremy was a member who had never shared much about his life, but that night he opened up about how he was HIV-positive and had contracted the disease through promiscuous relationships. To his shock, the group gathered around him, wept with him, embraced him and committed to stand with him. That night two visitors were present at the group. One woman stood up and stated, "This is not for me" and walked out. The other said, "If this is really the kind of people you are, I want to know more about this Jesus."

This book is about finding your own version of Sally's story. This is the story of what the Father-Son-Holy Spirit is doing in the midst of the world to restore life, community and his mission of love. Whether you lead a small group of ten that meets in your home, a creative group that meets in a coffee shop, or a missional community of twenty-five to thirty, what follows introduces the key leadership practices that will move your group from being a "good" meeting group to one that participates with Jesus in a way that changes life as we know it and shines forth the surprising and unexpected way of God's kingdom. This is a story that God is writing in you, through you and around you. Welcome to the way of Jesus.

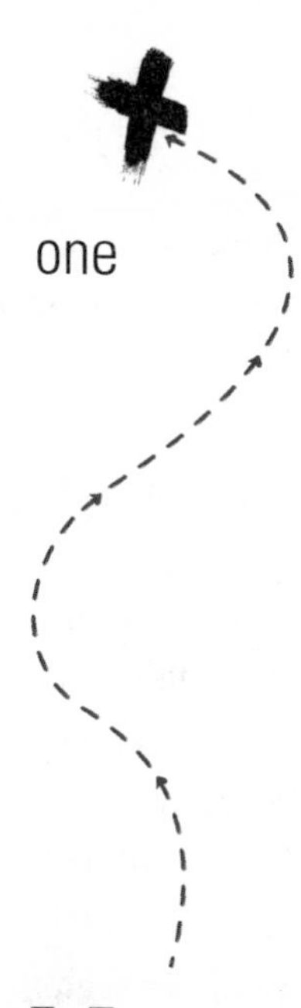

one

The Search for Great Group Leadership

Nothing in this physical world has influenced my life like other people have. As I look back on the steps I have taken with Jesus, I think about friends like Gavin, Jackson, Scott, Terry, Greg, Bryan, Janice and Mary. Mentors like Brenda, Mike, Joey, Alan and Jim come to mind. Those I have mentored like John, Jenny, Phil, Darrin and Mike have affected me more than I affected them. Then of course there is my wife Shawna, who has shaped my life more than anyone.

People have changed who I am. We are shaped relationally. We are not isolated nomads who define ourselves apart from others. We are who we are today in large part because of the shoulders we have rubbed.

As I think about various people who have influenced me, I realize that all of these relationships developed in small group contexts of some kind. One-on-one relationships never occur without some kind of small group horizon as a backdrop. Some groups are formal and organized while others develop informally.

Groups shape who we are. They form us to see the world from a particular point of view, whether we acknowledge it or not. And most of the time we don't recognize it because groups permeate just about every aspect of our lives. We are born into a small group called a family. We go to school in small groups called classes. We play sports in small groups called teams. We make money in jobs as a part of small groups called departments. Small groups are everywhere.

Through the years I have searched high and low for New Testament commands to join a small group in the church. (This would, after all, help me promote this book.) Try as I might, however, I've yet to find that meeting in small groups was ever commanded. Instead, small group life was presumed by the writers of the Bible; it was the normative way of doing things in their culture, just as it has been throughout history. For instance, Hebrews 10:24-25 reads, "And let us consider how we may spur one another on toward love and good deeds, not giving up meeting together, as some are in the habit of doing, but encouraging one another—and all the more as you see the Day approaching."

When the author of Hebrews wrote this he was imagining a house church of some kind. He was not talking about attending a church meeting at an official church building at an official church time led by an official church speaker, like we think about today. (Please note that I do not mean this as a judgment against what occurs today in our church buildings on Sundays. I'm only saying that the New Testament mode of operation of church was different.) The author's imagination about "meeting together" was shaped by the experience of small groups formed in relational, organic ways.

While small groups are never prescribed in the New Testament, they are obviously central to the ministry of Jesus—he primarily ministered to and with a small group of twelve disciples—and that of the early church, whose members primarily met from "house to house" (Acts 20:20). The gospel spreads through small groups. The way of Jesus is a way of small groups.

The question for us is, how do we lead our groups well? And more specifically, when it comes to leading groups of God's people, how do we lead others in the way of Jesus? Whether it's a small group, a cell group, a home group, a missional small group, a missional community or a house church . . . whether we meet in a home, in a conference room at our workplace, at a restaurant or even at the church building . . . whether we use a Bible study guide, read a book together, talk about our pastor's sermon or get together to discuss how God is moving in our life . . . the question for all of us is the same: How do we lead people in the way of Jesus?

My search for answers to this question has been driven by three conversations with leaders who asked these questions of me. All three loved God. All three wanted to serve God in the way they led. They wanted to be great at their jobs in God's eyes. However, the specific questions that arose during our conversations illustrate three common barriers that can keep us from leading people in the way of Jesus.

THE IDEAL PERSONALITY?

I met Jim for coffee at a local restaurant. He and his wife, Julie, had been a part of the Halls' group for about four years. When I started overseeing groups at this church, the Halls were repeatedly brought to my attention. Their group was held up as the ideal. And after I got to know them I understood why. They were the kind of people others just wanted to be around: winsome, welcoming, hospitable and wise. They were also fun and giving, and they knew how to pray for others and lead groups to pray for each other. I got to know the Halls very well, and I will be forever grateful for their friendship.

Jim and Julie were grateful also. But they were venturing out and starting a new group, and they expressed concerns. Jim asked something like this: "How can we lead like the Halls? We're so different from them. We don't have their infectious personalities.

They're 'people' people. We tend to be more introverted. They have lots of life experience. We're young. They have space to host gatherings. We live in a small apartment that makes it hard to entertain. They just have the right gifts that make for great small group leaders. How do we do what they do?"

Jim's questions for me that day reflect a common assumption people make about leading groups: that some people are wired to lead well and others are not. Some, like the Halls, have the right mix of personality, spiritual gifts and personal talents that make small group leadership easy. The rest of us must try to be more like them.

I wish I were immune to this assumption. When we see an effective leader it's tempting to measure ourselves against him or her. Of course, this leads us nowhere except into self-evaluation and, usually, self-condemnation. For the few of us who might be an exception, it can lead to puffed-up pride.

The reality is that Jim and Julie could in no way be like the Halls. And there was no need for them to try. Multiple research projects have demonstrated that no one personality makes for a better leader. No mix of spiritual gifts stands out as being better suited to leading well. In addition, attributes like the leader's gender, social class, age, marital status and education have no bearing on one's ability to effectively lead a group.[1] Simply put, the Halls are not the ideal model for small group leadership because no such thing exists.

As soon as you or anyone else holds up some kind of predetermined icon of how a group leader should look or act, you will miss the way that God wants to uniquely move through you.

Even worse, a falsely held ideal of leadership hinders us from growing into who God has made us to be as unique individuals. The way another leader leads cannot be duplicated. You are not that other leader. Small group leadership is not about reproducing widget-like leaders who all fall in line with a predetermined ideal. We are called to grow in our ability to be ourselves, to lead out of our identity as uniquely formed children of God. While I can learn from other leaders, I cannot mimic what they do.

THE IDEAL VISION?

The second conversation from my years mentoring small group leaders occurred with a single man in his early twenties named Robert. Robert was probably the most eager and committed leader I ever worked with. He loved his group and spent a lot of energy investing in his members. One afternoon we were sitting at my house going through some basic ideas about group leadership. He asked me a simple question: What should be my focus as a leader? I told him what one of my mentors had told me. Small group leadership is simply about having a clear vision for three things: Love God. Love people. Make disciples who love God and love people.

Robert's eyes lit up. We talked about the Great Commission and the Great Commandment and how focusing on the purposes of the church found therein shape the life of an effective group. He left more focused than ever because he had great clarity of vision. He knew the destination for his group. All he had to do was head in that direction.

Robert lived out the focus on the Great Commission and the Great Commandment. And while I still believe what I told him that day, I've since come to realize that having clarity and focus of vision for a group will only get you going in the right direction. It won't in itself bring about the realization of that vision.

In many cases, vision clarity produces the opposite effect on leaders. Having the right focus can actually be exhausting. Many small group experts have taught over the years that great group leaders must be willing to put ten to fifteen hours per week into the effort. The subtle message has been, "Pull yourself up by the bootstraps and get committed to loving people like Jesus told us to do. *Just do it!* And your group will be great." In other words, group leaders are expected to work hard, pray hard and put in extra effort to guide people. Since they know what to do, all they have to do is "just do it."

A just-do-it attitude connected to focusing on the right vision is not really focus at all. It's a focus on the *need* to be focused, which is a distraction from the real things that can lead a group to actually accomplish the vision. Take sports as an example—specifically, NFL football. Every team has a goal of winning the Super Bowl. The vision is clear; this is a football player's Great Commission and Great Commandment. But good teams don't start the season talking about winning the Super Bowl. Good players and coaches don't talk about the teams they play down the road. They talk about the next game on the schedule.

The best teams take it a step further. They don't just think about the next game; they hone in on the job they have to do in each play and what it takes to do that job well. Bill Belichick, head coach of the New England Patriots, preaches the mantra "do your job." Don't worry about the game, the outcome of the game or what other players are or are not doing. Do your job in this next play.

As opposed to "just do it," which assumes that working hard while focusing on the ultimate vision is the crucial aspect of leadership, great small group leaders follow the "do your job" approach. The key then is to identify what it means for leaders to do their job so that we participate in the Jesus way. This causes us to shift our attention away from trying to make the Great Commission and Great Commandment happen on to becoming the kind of leaders who participate in God's activity in the world, which results in the Great Commission and the Great Commandment. The question then is, how do we participate in this?

IDEAL ACTIONS?

A third conversation from my past explores what it means to participate in God's activity in our groups and in the world. This dialogue occurred within my own soul. This is my story. I've had a unique opportunity; while I was in my early twenties, I began helping authors write on this topic as an editor. Behind the scenes I gained a wealth of knowledge about what it means to be a great small group leader.

About three years into this journey, I entered into group leadership at my church with gusto. I'd received the right training. I'd been mentored by an experienced group leader. I'd been involved in groups that flourished. I knew the actions that consistently led groups to live out the Great Commission and the Great Commandment. These included things like

- praying for your group members on a regular basis
- inviting people to your group
- contacting group members
- getting people involved in discussion
- raising up a new leader from within the group
- facilitating fellowship activities

I knew all the leadership actions that had been proven effective and produced results, and I did them. However, my group never came together as a community, and it failed to have any impact on others outside the group, even though everyone had a clear vision for both.

At the same time, I had a friend who was leading another group. He was doing all of the same things I was doing, but his group was flourishing. I wish I could say I rejoiced in his success but, alas, I must be honest—this frustrated me. So I redoubled my efforts. I performed the activities with even greater effort, to no avail.

Over the years I've talked with many pastors and group leaders who have confessed similar experiences. And in many cases they assumed that they just hadn't found the right combination of actions. So they looked for the next group innovation or new way of leading groups to provide a new strategy for leadership. And with this came a new list of actions. We need to figure out a new program. Or meet on a different night. Or study different material. Or take a break and start back up in a couple of months. Or meet as a smaller group. Or meet as a larger group. Or . . . Or . . . I've even heard some leaders say they've just never figured out the right formula for small groups.

The search for the right leadership formula is the essence of the problem. There is no ideal program that provides the ideal list of ideal actions. Small group leadership is not a franchise model. A standardized approach works for training people at McDonald's, but small groups are about people, not French fries. God is at work in the world, and God works through relationships. We cannot make a fail-proof list for group leadership. We need more. We need to think in terms of leading so that we discover how to join God in what God is doing in those relationships.

REFRAMING LEADERSHIP GREATNESS

No small group leader I've ever met wants to do his or her job poorly. I've yet to encounter any who want to be merely mediocre. You are not reading this book because you want to be average or lead a normal group. You want to do your job well. You want a group that lives out the way of Jesus.

To get on this path, small group leaders must move beyond the three common barriers that hinder us. The search for the ideal personality, the ideal vision and the ideal actions will send us off on detours that might look like the way of Jesus but in reality have little in common with it. We need to reframe leadership greatness so that our way of leading begins to reflect the way of Jesus. For this, Jesus does not give us much in the way of vision clarity or specific actions. Instead Jesus specialized in telling stories and using metaphors, one of which can help us see leadership as he did.

THE WAY OF SHEPHERDING

The metaphor of sheep and shepherding is crucial to understanding Jesus' way of leading. The Bible describes Jesus as the good shepherd (John 10:11). Matthew 9:36-38 reads, "When he saw the crowds, he had compassion on them, because they were harassed and helpless, like sheep without a shepherd. Then he said to his disciples, 'The harvest is plentiful but the workers are few. Ask the Lord of the harvest, therefore, to send out workers into his harvest field.'" The interesting thing is that this passage come right after a verse that reads, "Jesus went through all the towns and villages, teaching in their synagogues, proclaiming the good news of the kingdom and healing every disease and sickness" (Matthew 9:35). During the time of Jesus' ministry on earth, Jesus could not shepherd everyone by himself. He needed others to help him care for the scattered sheep. He needed shepherds who would be with the sheep and guide them in his way.

Likewise, Peter wrote, "Be shepherds of God's flock that is under your care, watching over them—not because you must, but because you are willing, as God wants you to be; not pursuing dishonest gain, but eager to serve; not lording it over those entrusted to you, but being examples to the flock" (1 Peter 5:2-3).

Most people today don't have any experience with sheep. However, I grew up tending a flock on my dad's farm, so I've had many conversations in response to the question, "What does it mean for small group leaders to be shepherds?" The original audiences of Scripture would have had a thorough knowledge of sheep and shepherding. Even if they did not have firsthand experience, they knew others who did or they had observed the life of sheep and shepherds in their villages. After all, sheep were as common then as smartphones are today.

The parable of the lost sheep in Luke 15 can help us enter into the imagination of Jesus about leadership. It reads:

> Now the tax collectors and sinners were all gathering around to hear Jesus. But the Pharisees and the teachers of the law muttered, "This man welcomes sinners and eats with them."
>
> Then Jesus told them this parable: "Suppose one of you has a hundred sheep and loses one of them. Doesn't he leave the ninety-nine in the open country and go after the lost sheep until he finds it? And when he finds it, he joyfully puts it on his shoulders and goes home. Then he calls his friends and neighbors together and says, 'Rejoice with me; I have found my lost sheep.' I tell you that in the same way there will be more rejoicing in heaven over one sinner who repents than over ninety-nine righteous persons who do not need to repent." (Luke 15:1-7)

Jesus told parables in response to a situation. In this case, Jesus was eating with "tax collectors" and "sinners." The first group was composed of notoriously dishonest men who had aligned themselves with Rome, the enemy of Israel. The second label was for those who, for a variety of reasons, had been excluded from fellowship with the supposed "righteous" members of the community. These "sinners" were not necessarily those who practiced immorality, but they may have been so poor that they had no means to know the law or try to keep it. As a result, they were religious outcasts. One such group of people who were labeled "sinners" were shepherds.

The Pharisees and legal experts were grumbling because of this meal sharing. To understand why they were so upset, we need to understand the honor expressed in sharing a meal in Jesus' time. To invite someone to share a meal was to extend peace, trust, brotherhood and forgiveness. It was a way of saying that another person was valued. In addition, the text implies that Jesus actually hosted meals for tax collectors and sinners. This would have been even more offensive than casually going to a sinner's home. The host had a specific role at the meal in this culture. As the host Jesus would have complimented his guests, thereby honoring them around the table.

In response to the grumbling, Jesus told the parable of the lost sheep. He opened by saying, "Suppose one of you has a hundred sheep . . . " Such a comment to the religiously pure would have been offensive because they did not own sheep; shepherding was an impure profession. To address his audience as "shepherds" implied that these men of means, these leaders of the community, these supposed insiders in the things of God were supposed to be shepherds who cared for God's people. They were supposed to be servants of those in need. Ezekiel 34 goes into great depth about God's expectations for Israel's leaders to be shepherds to his people. The Old Testament prophet wrote about what the leaders of Israel failed to do:

> This is what the Sovereign LORD says: Woe to you shepherds who only care of yourselves! Should not the shepherds take care of the flock? You eat curds, clothe yourselves with the wool and slaughter the choice animals, but you do not take care of the flock. You have not strengthened the weak or healed the sick or bound up the injured. You have not brought back the strays or searched for the lost. You have ruled them harshly and brutally. So they were scattered because there was no shepherd, and when they were scattered they became food for all the wild animals. My sheep wandered over all the mountains and on every high hill. They were scattered over the whole earth, and no one searched or looked for them. (Ezekiel 34:2-6)

Likewise, the leaders of Israel in Jesus' day failed to understand God's call on them to be shepherds. In this parable, there are a hundred sheep. This would have been a large flock, as the average family would have had only five to fifteen sheep. Normally the owner of that many sheep would hire workers to attend his flock, but here the owner goes out himself to find the lost sheep. This is a direct challenge to the leaders of Israel to participate in God's call to embrace those on the outside.

Shepherds usually work in pairs with flocks this size. When they realize a sheep is lost, one shepherd takes the flock back home while the other seeks the misplaced one. Experienced shepherds say lost sheep will lie down helplessly and refuse to budge. They are overcome by a sense of hopelessness and need someone to find them and save them. Once the shepherd finds a lost sheep, he must carry the animal a long distance.

In Jesus' parable, when the first shepherd returned with the ninety-nine sheep, the neighbors would have noticed the other shepherd's absence. There would have been great concern for the safety of the searching shepherd along with concern for the sheep. In that culture people within villages and towns were a connected community. A lost sheep or shepherd was a loss to the whole village. The recovery of the sheep would have been an occasion of joy for all.

When Jesus told this parable he was not holding up an ideal model for what it meant to be a good leader. He did not lay out a clear vision. Nor did he provide a list of actions that the leaders should implement.

He told a story that chipped away at the hardness of his listeners' hearts. He used a metaphor that bored into their souls. These were not leaders who

- took care of others
- strengthened the weak
- healed the sick
- brought back the strays
- searched for the lost

Shepherding in such a way is a matter of heart. It goes far beyond getting the job done. While I was growing up on the farm I did not have the heart of a shepherd, but I saw someone who did: my father. Whereas I threw rocks at the sheep to scare them into the pen—which never worked—my father had only to open the gate and they came running. I would wait to tend to them until it was convenient for me; my father would consistently care and watch over them no matter what the cost to himself. I barely knew the differences among them, but my father remembered details about the last lamb of each ewe and when she was expected to give birth again.

That day Jesus confronted the practices of the supposed leaders of the people of God and offered an alternative. Today we must hear this challenge and embrace the alternative, making room for the Spirit to shape our souls to be shepherds in the way of Jesus.

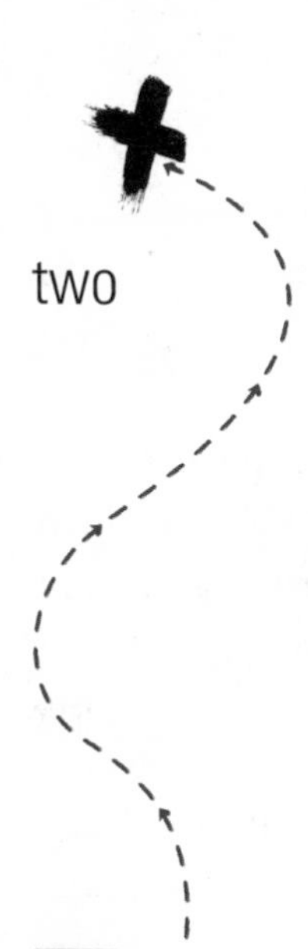

Leading in the Way of Jesus

Tomorrow when you awake, you will follow a rather predictable set of habits. You won't necessarily think about your actions or plan them out. Rather, because you have repeated the same steps so many times, you will take part in your internalized routine without thinking about it. Most of us drive home from work on the same set of roads every day. Do you ever pull into the driveway and think, *How did I get here*? There are complex scientific reasons that tell us how this route has been burned into our brains to such a degree that we don't have to overtly think about it.[1]

Habits shape almost every aspect of every day. The way we start the day, how we interact with family and coworkers, how we eat our meals and how we end our days are all shaped by habits that we don't even recognize. Researchers have performed extensive analysis on how habits work, and they have come to recognize that a habit is much more than a repeated action. It's more complex than the fact that I drink coffee every morning. Drinking the coffee is a practice that shapes my internalized routines. A habit is most easily understood as a loop with three basic parts: a cue, a practice and a reward. All three must be in place for a habit to form. A cue initiates a practice that results in some kind of reward or desired outcome. At the most basic level, we see this at play in how we eat. Hunger is the cue that sparks the routine of eating, which results in the reward of satisfaction. This satisfaction, in turn, reinforces the cue.

If we want different results in our life, we have to change the habit loop. It's not enough to identify a habit and simply work hard at trying to change it. For instance, if you want to get in shape, you must develop a habit of exercising. This will require the identification of a cue—like the alarm clock going off or putting on shorts when you get home from work—and then give yourself some kind of reward at the end of exercising, such as sitting in the whirlpool or treating yourself to a fruit smoothie. The cue then points to the practice and the reward reinforces the cue. The goal is to change the practice so that we create a new internalized habit.

This habit loop relates to almost every area of life. The cue to begin working might be the clock striking nine o'clock or walking into an office. These cues initiate our practices at work. For me this involves specific actions related to the computer, including writing, editing and some artistic design work. The reward or outcome could be the satisfaction from the work completed or the income generated from the work. For some, it might include the praise from a boss or a client or the potential of a promotion.

This same habit loop relates to the way we lead. We all lead in ways that we don't recognize as habitual. Leaders who talk too much in group meetings often don't know that they're doing so. Those who come across as controlling might very well intend to be caring. A leader might think that he has led a great meeting because he followed the Bible study the pastor gave him, but in fact he's followed the same pattern so closely that everything is predictable. All of us have unrecognized leadership habits. Some are helpful; others keep us from the outcomes we desire.

If we want to change the nature of the outcomes in our group, we have to change the practices that the cues initiate. As Albert

Einstein purportedly said, "The definition of insanity is doing the same thing while expecting different results." We cannot redouble our efforts at what we are already doing and expect to get different outcomes. In the chapters that follow, I introduce eight practices that I have found helpful in breaking us out of habits that undermine groups. These are practices that honor the call to lead as a shepherd in the way of Jesus.

These practices will help us break patterns of "insanity" so that we can expect to get different outcomes from our leadership. But here's the catch. Most likely, these are not the practices we would expect. At least they're not the practices I expected to write about when I began to do the research to write this book. I expected to provide a clear, concrete list of tasks that we can adopt in order to be a better leader. But as I stated earlier, this approach leads us astray. The search for ideal actions leads us to depend on techniques. And leading people (sheep) requires more than a set of techniques.

TECHNIQUES ARE NOT ENOUGH

Most of the time, when we think of what we can do to get different results, we think in terms of techniques. We live in a world driven by techniques. If you have a problem, someone out there has a solution they're willing to sell you. If you follow their secret knowledge, then you'll get different results. If you want to make money, there's a plan for that. If you want to be happy, then follow the steps some expert outlines for you. If you want to make something happen, someone has developed a technique that promises to get it for you.

This technique mindset has infiltrated the church more than any of us would like to admit. It works like this: if you want to experience x, then follow the a + b + c formula. Examples are endless: pray the right prayer and you'll see your finances turn around; believe the right set of doctrines and you'll find God's favor; proclaim the right promises of God and you'll find success in your job. I think one of the most comical formulas I ever heard was at a Valentine's Day banquet. After the guest pastor told all kinds of funny stories from his thirty years of counseling troubled marriages, he told us the secret to a great marriage. He said, "Every night before you go to bed, strip down naked and kneel beside the bed and pray together." He promised that this formula works every time. I don't think that any further comment is needed.

Small group leadership resources are not immune to this focus on techniques. These techniques usually sound something like the following:

- four steps to leading a great small group discussion
- three keys to building community
- seven ways to pray for your group members
- six rules for leading worship in groups
- five ways to reach the community with the gospel
- how to ask great questions that generate discussion
- how to contact group members between meetings
- a surefire strategy for developing a new leader

For instance, statistical research has been conducted demonstrating that group leaders who spend more time with God on a daily basis lead groups that grow faster.[2] So I and others teach this key to great group leadership: spend an hour per day in daily devotions. If you do this, then your group will take off. Other techniques like this have been offered through the years. The assumption is that if you just do a + b + c then you will be a great leader and guide your group into the land of promise.

While there is a place for group leadership techniques—I've written and continue to write in that vein—it's just not enough. I would argue it's not even the place to start when it comes to great group experiences. Most of the things that lead groups into great experiences do not depend on our ability to do a technique properly. While how-to training is a good thing, real breakthroughs in people's lives almost always call for something other than technique.

For instance, consider how to open a meeting in a way that gets people involved. One of the best ways to do this is to use an icebreaker. Small group research and experience have repeatedly shown that icebreakers help people warm up to one another and to discussions. And there are some technical rules for leading an icebreaker well. These rules include:

- Ask open-ended, nonthreatening questions that draw out people's interests and experiences.
- Have the leader answer the question first to get the conversation moving and model how to answer in a short fashion.
- Go around in a circle.
- If people want to give long responses, remind them that icebreakers call for short answers so that everyone can participate.
- If people want to pass, allow them to do so. Don't force people to respond.

Do this according to the rules, and you find that people open up more naturally and quickly. But technique will get you only so far in certain situations.

At one time I led a group where Barry always passed when it was his turn to respond to the icebreaker. In fact, he would sit in the meeting every week without saying a word. Whatever I tried, he would not open up. The rule about allowing people to pass is meant to be rarely used. Barry was turning it into the norm. He told other members that he loved the group and was growing in his walk with Jesus, but his lack of participation was creating discomfort with others in the group. And there was no technique that was going to get Barry to open up. I did not know the real issue that kept him from sharing, and I did not have any clear solutions. Try as I might, I could not get him to participate.

This experience brings me back to the biblical theme of sheep. I had to learn to see Barry for who he was just as a shepherd develops skills to see his sheep.

SEE THE SHEEP

The last conversation between Jesus and Peter reads:

> When they had finished eating, Jesus said to Simon Peter, "Simon son of John, do you love me more than these?"
>
> "Yes, Lord," he said, "you know that I love you."
>
> Jesus said, "Feed my lambs."
>
> Again Jesus said, "Simon son of John, do you love me?"
>
> He answered, "Yes, Lord, you know that I love you."
>
> Jesus said, "Take care of my sheep."
>
> The third time he said to him, "Simon son of John, do you love me?"
>
> Peter was hurt because Jesus asked him the third time, "Do you love me?" He said, "Lord, you know all things; you know that I love you."
>
> Jesus said, "Feed my sheep." (John 21:15-17)

Leading groups in the way of Jesus is a call to feed God's sheep. If we do this, the sheep will naturally and organically grow and move toward a life that fulfills the vision of the Great Commission and the Great Commandment. Feeding the sheep well is the outcome of the leadership practices we develop. If we are going to do this, then we need to understand a bit more about sheep.

I grew up on a family farm in North Texas where we raised everything from cows to chickens, rabbits to turkeys. We stayed away from pigs and horses, but just about every other farm animal called our farm home at some point. And the species that seemed to impact our lives the most was the sheep. While we owned more cattle, the small flock of sheep was part of our lives more than any other type of animal we raised.

Unlike cattle, sheep require up-close-and-personal care. For instance, sheep lack the ability to regulate how much they eat. If food is out, they will eat it. And if they eat too much, they will die. In addition, they have sensitive stomachs. So a shepherd must feed them the right amount of the right food.

Also, sheep have no ability to protect themselves. They are frail and slow, and they cannot kick, claw or bite. They are easily spooked. They will scatter in panic and, once cornered, sit petrified while staring at their predator. A shepherd is required to protect them. This is why sheep must be penned at night and watched over by day. On our farm the field in which the sheep ran during the day was protected by good fences to keep out dogs and other predators, but we still penned them up every evening.

Sheep give birth to little lambs, which are truly the cutest things in the world. However, the lambing season falls in the winter. When it was time for the ewes on our farm to give birth, we had to watch them closely. I cannot count the late nights when my dad would put on his coat "one more time" and head out to the barn to check if any new lambs were about to enter the world. They often needed help getting up so they could take their first milk, especially on cold days and nights.

Sheep are loud. They are intellectually challenged (scientific fact). They are prone to wander off. They stink. Oh my, do they stink. Just imagine four inches of wool at the end of a long rainy winter. Sheep are the only farm animal that requires annual shearing. This can be a good thing because it provides a source of income, but it also illustrates the kind of special care a shepherd provides that is not required for other animals. This one biological characteristic demonstrates how sheep cannot live on their own. If somehow sheep got smarter and developed the ability to protect themselves, they still could not survive in the wild. If the wool were not shorn, it would grow so long that it would get top heavy. Then when it got wet, they would fall over, legs flailing. They would die helplessly waiting for a shepherd to come and turn them over.

One more thing: sheep cannot be driven. It's not easy to force them to go anywhere. If you drive them, they will scatter. In his book *They Smell Like Sheep*, Lynn Anderson tells the story of a tour he was leading in Israel where he was teaching people about the ancient practices of shepherding. While talking, he looked out the window of the tour bus and saw a man driving sheep. He was irate and told the bus driver to stop. He walked over to the man and told him how shepherds were not supposed to drive sheep. The man responded, "I'm not a shepherd. I'm a *butcher*!"[3]

While shepherding techniques can be helpful, much more is required to deal with the problems and challenges of working with animals like this. And there is a reason that Scripture uses the metaphor of sheep to describe humans. We are weak and in need of special care.

DISCOVERY AND ADAPTATION

In order to lead sheep well, we must understand the kinds of problems sheep face so we can find appropriate solutions to those problems. The solutions are connected to three different kinds of actions. We've already discussed the first: technique. The second action is discovery, and the third is adaptation. Table 2.1 illustrates the differences.[4]

Table 2.1. Appropriate responses to three kinds of problems

Kind of Action	Problem	Solution	Source
Technique	Clearly understood	Known	Group leader
Discovery	Clearly understood	Known by someone	Leader and group
Adaptation	Unknown	Unknown	Group

Leadership techniques work when a problem is clear and the leader knows the solution.[5] Small group leadership techniques are valuable in situations where the kind of leadership called for is straightforward. For example, as we discussed earlier, leaders who pray in daily devotions and in intercession for their group members lead better groups. So we do well to develop our time with God and pray. There are also clear techniques for how to lead effective meetings, create social events and reach people who don't know Jesus.

But groups also face challenges where the solutions are not clear. The problem might be obvious but the leader has no idea what to do. Someone else might know a solution, but the entire group must collaborate to draw it out. This is the leadership action focused on discovery.

Then there are times when the problems are not clear at all. The solutions are also unknown, and the group has to adapt as they follow God's leading along the way.

Most of the time, when we are frustrated by challenges that require discovery or adaptation, we look for answers from authorities, hoping someone "in charge" will provide a strategy to solve the problem we face. Leaders feel the pressure to act, to make something different happen and thereby overcome the problem. So they turn to a spiritual expert—usually someone with the title "pastor"—to give them a clear path to turn things around. Then the leader acts.

But groups are about people and people bring with them challenges. When we look for answers from an authority, more frustrations inevitably arise, creating a perpetual loop of frustration. Ronald Heifetz, an expert in adaptive leadership, writes, "In response to our frustration, we are likely to perpetuate the vicious cycle by looking *even more earnestly* to authority, but this time we look for someone new offering more certainty and better promises."[6]

No expert or spiritual authority had any insight into helping Barry open up during the meetings I was leading. In fact, if we had turned to an authority, we probably would have driven Barry further away. Our challenge called for creative collaboration. There was no magical thing that any one person did. We prayed. Different members talked to him outside the meeting, increasing his level of trust. We laughed. Simply put, we created an environment where we could relate to one another well. We talked about the challenges we faced and sometimes came up with solutions. Most often the solutions arose over time. In other words, we learned as we went along. Then one day Barry answered the icebreaker. About three weeks later he shared when we were discussing the Scriptures. Barry did not fit any predetermined plan. We had to meet him as a person and adapt along the way.

IT TAKES PRACTICE

Some leaders have an innate ability to see the way of Jesus and practice those things that align with it. Perhaps their personality fits their way of leading, their history has shaped them to move in this direction, or the school of hard knocks has formed relational character. Whatever the reason, it just comes naturally to them.

But most of us are not there yet. We must develop spiritual disciplines or practices that shape us for the journey. Tim Morey writes in his book *Embodying Our Faith*, "A spiritual discipline is any practice that enables a person to do through training what he or she is not able to do simply by trying. They are practices, relationships and experiences that bring our minds and bodies into cooperation with God's work in our lives, making us more capable of receiving more of his life and power."[7]

We practice our way into discovery and adaptive action.[8] We cannot will ourselves into it. If we want to develop a skill like horseback riding, graphic design or sailing, we have do the stuff that teaches us how to do it. The way we do this is to practice. As Craig Dykstra and Dorothy Bass note, "Christian practices are things

Christian people do together over time in response to and in the light of God's active presence for the life of the world in Christ Jesus."[9] The practices of leading create space in our lives and with other people so that the way of Jesus can come to life. According to Dykstra, "They are patterns of communal action that create openings in our lives where the grace, mercy and presence of God may be known to us. They are places where the power of God is experienced. In the end, these are not ultimately our practices but forms of participation in the practice of God."[10] These practices train us to move beyond leading as if we were the agents of change to participating in the work of God, who is the acting agent in our groups.

Practice requires attention, focus, concentrated repetition and effort in the early stages. Over time this changes us. The practices move beyond things we do. In a way, they become part of us. "After a time, the primary point about the practice is no longer that they are something we do," Dykstra notes. "Instead, they become arenas in which something is done to us, in us, and through us that we could not of ourselves do, that is beyond what we do."[11] We learn to do them without having to think because they have become habits.[12]

WHAT PRACTICES PRODUCE

Practices possess within them the seed or DNA of the end that is envisioned. If the end is making money, then we adopt practices that line up with that end. The practices are done for the sake of making money. If the end is winning in a sport, like basketball, then the player adopts practices that line up with winning basketball games. There are other practices that might make a person a better athlete, but the DNA of winning at basketball is not present in all of them. The end dictates the nature of the athlete's practices.

The end we envision for our small groups will dictate the kinds of practices we adopt as leaders. Over the years there have been many different "ends" offered for small groups or missional communities. They include things like evangelism, discipleship, getting people connected, Bible study, multiplication of groups, or creating a Jesus movement. Those with the goal of evangelistic growth will focus on practices to reach the lost. Those that seek Bible study will spend great effort honing their Bible study skills.

Over the years I've wondered if the apostle Paul might write something like this today: "If my group reaches lost people and grows but there is no love, we are only a growing shell of emptiness. If my group raises up new leaders and multiplies but there is no love, we are only multiplying a form of spiritual cancer. If my group gets serious about discipleship and dives deep into the Word but there is no love, we are puffed up hoarders of information. If my group serves and goes forth on mission but there is no love, we are like a chicken with its head cut off. If my group gets lots of people in my church connected but there is no love, we are no better than a salesperson who sells products for a living."

This is my modern interpretation of Paul's opening words in his famous love chapter:

> If I speak in the tongues of men or of angels, but do not have love, I am only a resounding gong or a clanging cymbal. If I have the gift of prophecy and can fathom all mysteries and all knowledge, and if I have a faith that can move mountains, but do not have love, I am nothing. If I give all I possess to the poor and give over my body to hardship that I may boast, but do not have love, I gain nothing. (1 Corinthians 13:1-3)

Paul's point then and my point now is that our actions, our goals, our vision and even our results matter little if we don't have love, because love defines the way of Jesus.

The way of Jesus defines the nature of our practices. The practices are shaped by the essence of who God is and, as 1 John 4:8 states, "God is love." Love is at the core of God's being. However, love is a complicated subject. All I have to do is to reflect on the movies that informed my teenage years. From *The Breakfast Club* to *Pretty in Pink*, love is depicted as the mysterious connection between two forlorn beings who are hoping to find that magic moment. Illustrations of various kinds of love are endless. Songs, books, television shows and movies impact our imaginations because they tell stories. Stories shape how we think and live. And there is no other topic about which more stories are told than the topic of love. Whether it's love of baseball, love for a friend, love for children, the love of money and power, or love for God, this four-letter word makes for good stories. So when we read the words "God is love," most of us have tons of backstory through which we interpret this statement.

Much of this backstory is the up-close-and-personal kind. Some people were told by their father that he loved them, but what they experienced was distance, anger and maybe even worse. When they hear, "God loves you" or "The Father's heart is full of love for you," the backstory that fills their imagination makes this hard to believe. As a result, the words "God is love" are little more than abstract theology. Understanding God as a relational God depends on our personal story of receiving love. We will relate to others the way we have experienced God's relationship with us.

For instance, if we view God as a demanding tyrant, we will offer love out of fear of getting caught if we don't. Like a subject in a cruel dictator's domain, we will do what God wants because we don't want to endure the pain of his wrath. Then we will love others the same way. If we view God as a distant, disinterested deity, we will love God in a similar fashion, without passion or intimacy. Then we will love others the same way. If we view God as a nice Santa Claus figure who gives us gifts but is not involved in our lives on a daily basis, then our love for him will likewise be sporadic. And we will love others the same way.[13]

We love because God first loved us (1 John 4:19). Therefore, love of others is an overflow of our love received from God. I don't mean this in abstract terms, as in when we make orthodox statements regarding how much Jesus demonstrated his love for us on the cross. I'm referring to the experience of God's love. Love is not love if it's abstract. Love is about encounter. We are relational only because we have experienced God's relational love for us. Too often we forget this. We focus so much on the lists of things a Christian should and should not do that we fail to see that we love only because we have first experienced God's love.

We need to fill the word *love* with God's backstory if we are going to receive and experience the kind of love that God is. God gets to define the way that he loves. We don't. "This is how we know what love is: Jesus Christ laid down his life for us. And we ought to lay down our lives for our brothers and sisters" (1 John 3:16).

The cross is the revelation of God's love. We need to fill our imaginations with that story so we can overcome all the other stories that provide mistaken notions of love. Crosslike love reveals who God is. But that kind of love is hard to fathom, especially from a god. We don't naturally envision or desire a deity who allows himself to suffer and die while being totally misunderstood. What kind of love is that? It's such a wild story that it either reframes everything or has no impact at all. This is exactly the kind of God revealed in Jesus, and Jesus reveals what God looks like. God is relational through and through because of the way the Father, Son and Spirit relate to one another. Theologian John Franke puts it this way:

> The statement "God is love" refers primarily to the eternal, relational, intratrinitarian fellowship among Father, Son, and Holy Spirit, who together are the one God. In this way, God is love within the divine reality, and in this sense, through all eternity, God is the social Trinity, the community of love.[14]

The way of Jesus is the way of love demonstrated on the cross. The practices of Jesus' way will be practices that train us to "take up [our] cross daily and follow [him]" (Luke 9:23).

Think of how this contrasts with our normal patterns of relating. Our world most often trains us in practices where we value ourselves at the expense of others. The way of Jesus love turns this around: we value others at expense to ourselves.[15]

Paul's words in 1 Corinthians 13 call us into this relational way. These are not merely words meant for wedding ceremonies. These are words for the church. Because they have been quoted so often, I find that hearing them from a fresh perspective like that of Eugene Peterson's *The Message* is helpful:

> Love never gives up.
> Love cares more for others than for self.
> Love doesn't want what it doesn't have.
> Love doesn't strut,
> Doesn't have a swelled head,
> Doesn't force itself on others,
> Isn't always "me first,"
> Doesn't fly off the handle,
> Doesn't keep score of the sins of others,
> Doesn't revel when others grovel,
> Takes pleasure in the flowering of truth,
> Puts up with anything,
> Trusts God always,
> Always looks for the best,
> Never looks back,
> But keeps going to the end.[16]

When we talk about leading in the way of Jesus, we are simply talking about becoming the kind of leaders who live in the love of God demonstrated on the cross, allowing God's love to move through us. The end is God's love, and since God loves the world (John 3:16), we are simply joining him in the continuing work of the Spirit to love the world with crosslike love. We need leadership practices that will align us with how God's Spirit is moving. We are creating environments in our groups so that people can grow in this crosslike love. This is the end. This is the goal.

WHY DIDN'T SOMEONE TELL ME THIS?

I wish someone had sat me down and pumped into my head this one truth about training leaders to love before they started giving me lessons on the technical aspects of leading groups. If someone had done that—or if I had listened if someone did say it to me—it would have spared me a lot of stress. Instead of struggling to figure out what I was doing wrong in my implementation of leadership techniques, I would have known the limitations of those techniques. This is not to belittle the technical side of group leadership. We just need to recognize its proper place.

Of course, no one starts out with the ability to love like Jesus. We need practices that equip and guide us along the way. Over the years I've observed that those who grow in crosslike love engage in a common set of practices. They include:

- Practice 1: Hear the rhythms of the Jesus way
- Practice 2: Gather in the presence
- Practice 3: Lead collaboratively
- Practice 4: Be yourself
- Practice 5: Hang out
- Practice 6: Make a difference
- Practice 7: Fight well
- Practice 8: Point the way to the cross

This is not meant to be a list of things we do, a list that replaces other lists that describe what small groups leaders do. These practices do not work when we treat them in an "a + b + c = great leadership" way. When we do this, we turn the way of Jesus into something we produce. The way of Jesus is already happening in the world. These practices are meant to help us step on to the way and participate in what God is doing in our world.

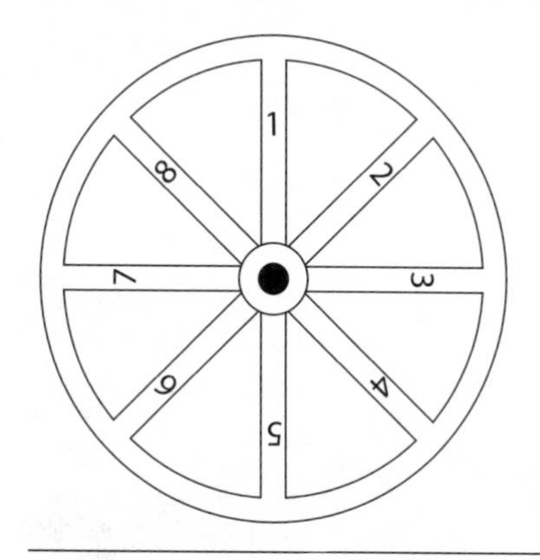

1: Hear the rhythms of the Jesus way
2: Gather in the presence
3: Lead collaboratively
4: Be yourself
5: Hang out
6: Make a difference
7: Fight well
8: Point the way to the cross

Figure 2.1. Practices for growing in love

These eight practices are not developed in a linear fashion. They act like spokes on a wheel moving us forward. None of them comes before the others. Nor do we outgrow any of them. We never master them, as they are practices of a lifetime. In the early stages of our leadership development, the wheel may be small and move slowly. At times the spokes may be uneven so we move forward in a clunky manner. But as we follow Jesus and allow the Spirit to shape us, our ability to participate with God and walk with Jesus on his way expands. Our job is to put ourselves in a place where the Spirit of God can shape us in these practices.

three

Hear the Rhythms of the Jesus Way

The First Practice

After John was put in prison, Jesus went into Galilee, proclaiming the good news of God. 'The time has come,' he said. 'The kingdom of God has come near. Repent and believe the good news!'" (Mark 1:14-15).

Boom! These words are like Thor's hammer hitting the ground, sending ripples through time and space, announcing that everything is different. More than a sermon about how people can get saved and go to heaven when they die. Far beyond a proclamation about how to have a better life. While the afterlife and victorious living are part of these words of the kingdom, Jesus' way does not fit nicely into such categories. With Jesus, God intersected time with his own ways to change the course of history. This was about the fulfillment of God's dream for the world, for the beginning of his rule—justice, peace and his very own presence.

The way of Jesus manifests the kingdom. It propels people into the restoration of everything that exists, the turning of the tide of evil by the introduction of wholeness and goodness. This is the fullness of life where God's way, exemplified in triune love, is known in all things. Hear it!

God's kingdom has come.

God's wholeness is present.

God's love has pervaded the earth.

The way of Jesus has burst on the scene.

Boom!

Yes! Yes! Yes! Even as I write this my heart beats with anticipation. However, for those of us who've been around the church for a while, this announcement can sound nothing like the trembling ground from Thor's hammer. The words become old hat—normal religious phrases that have lost their meaning. Like a joke for which we already know the punch line, or a movie whose ending we've already seen, the "wow" factor of Jesus' way shifts from earthshaking thunder to mere background noise.

When we fail to hear the way for what it is, when we presume that we already know what it is because we've heard about it so many times, our walk with Jesus recedes into mediocrity. Discipleship become perfunctory. Church becomes routine. We become addicts of average. Small groups become rote meetings that we participate in because it's the right thing to do, or because we like studying the Bible, or because we want to be faithful.

Groups need someone who will hear the way differently, who will rock the boat and refuse to accept "good" as "good enough."

EARS TO HEAR, EYES TO SEE

For those who personally encountered Jesus two thousand years ago, Jesus' announcement would have stood out like a red stripe on a white wall. The way of Jesus was not something anyone would have expected. No one—this cannot be reiterated enough—*no one* could have predicted that God's way would look like self-sacrificial love hanging on a cross. The king the nation of Israel expected was not supposed to die.

The Israelites of the first century expected a normal king—their word for this was "Messiah," which is *christos* in the Greek New

Testament—but that's not what they got. And most did not see what was going on. John put it this way: "The true light that gives light to everyone was coming into the world. He was in the world, and though the world was made through him, the world did not recognize him. He came to that which was his own, but his own did not receive him" (John 1:9-11). They did not have ears to hear Jesus and his way.

Ears work on two levels. The first is obvious: healthy ears have the ability to receive sound waves and process them. This is hearing on a physical level. However, ears hear on another level that is much harder to quantify. A "trained ear" hears things most people miss. An orchestra instructor can hear things an untrained ear will not. A mother hears a tone in her child's voice that reveals distress. A man hears the laugh of his wife and his heart leaps.

This is what Jesus was referring to when he said, "Whoever has ears to hear, let them hear" (Mark 4:9). There were some who heard Jesus' words and saw Jesus' life and were able to recognize the way. Their ears had been prepared to hear what he was up to. But others were conditioned to hear only what was normal. They were trapped by the average.

Some call this "paradigm thinking." A paradigm is an interpretive grid that sets up expectations for what we hear and understand. For instance, the inventor of photocopying technology tried to sell the idea to Kodak because he assumed that the idea of taking pictures of text on paper and reproducing them would be of interest to a company whose business was all about pictures. But there was no film involved. So the idea did not fit Kodak's interpretive grid about how pictures were supposed to work.

Jesus announced the kingdom in a context where his audience had a paradigm about how the kingdom was supposed to work. The people of Galilee and Jerusalem had an interpretive grid that defined what a Messiah would look like. He would come with the authority of the sword and drive out the Romans, much like King David ruled and drove out Israel's enemies. He would rule with pomp to restore the glory of Israel as a nation, much like King Solomon did. And he would usher in the manifest presence of God in such a way that all would see that Israel was God's chosen nation.[1] Contemporaries of Jesus tried to live out their paradigm of the kingdom through four basic strategies:[2]

The strategy of realism. This was the strategy of the Sadducees and the Herodians. These two groups, each in their own way, asked, "What is possible within the circumstances at hand?" Since the Romans were in charge, they tried to make the best of things and work within the rules of the power brokers.

The strategy of radical violence. The Zealots took this approach. They sought to establish Israel by meeting the violence of the Romans with equivalent violence. They were training to drive out the Romans with power.

The strategy of the enclave. A group called the Essenses adopted this strategy. They withdrew to the desert to escape the pollution of the culture so they could set up the new kingdom of God in pure form.

The strategy of ideal religion. The Pharisees followed this pattern. While they lived among the populace, they established an ideal way of doing "church" that separated themselves from the culture at large. Their goal was to find the right way to serve God so that others would join them and thereby usher in the kingdom of God.

Jesus' strategies did not fit any of these paradigms and, as a result, most people did not have the ears to hear what Jesus was up to. Their paradigm rejected his kingdom paradigm. Jesus never viewed his calling as realistic, though there were times when people like the Sadducees tried to loop him into their agenda. He refused to be violent, even though Peter thought violence was the way when he cut off the soldier's ear. He never escaped from reality (we have no record of Jesus interacting with the Essenses, as it would have required him to enter the enclave to do so). And he confronted the myth that some kind of ideal religion would change things, in spite of the fact that the Pharisees worked hard to manipulate him for their own purposes.

I wish I could say these four groups were only present in Jesus' time. However, this is not the case. All four have woven their way into the church, and they live and breathe today. Their ways set up paradigms and expectations for the way groups should work. And they keep us mired in normal, average, predictable small group life.

Before I identify how these four ways infiltrate small group strategies, let me explain something about paradigms. We invest emotions into our paradigms. We naturally respond favorably to ideas that reinforce our paradigms. In other words, our emotions respond with pleasure when we read or hear something that reinforces what we already know, believe and practice. However, when someone challenges or criticizes our paradigm, our natural reaction is to feel threatened and get defensive. Anything we hear as a threat to an established paradigm we dismiss without explanation.

I must warn you that I'm not writing this book to reinforce established paradigms of small group leadership. I want to invite you into a conversation that challenges the status quo. I want to take what we have received that is valuable and build on that. If normal group life is enough for you, then keep doing what you're doing. But be aware: what follows is meant to challenge the normal paradigms of how we expect groups to work.

When I personally have found myself facing a new idea, I've found it helpful to prepare myself in order to limit my emotions' ability to control what I hear and don't hear. I tell myself that the person with the new idea is not attacking me or my identity, even though I may not agree with him or her. I also tell myself that listening to a challenge leveled against my established paradigm does not mean that everything is wrong about it. It just means that I have to consider the possibility that what I have been doing will not get me where I want to go.

Now back to how the four paradigms Jesus faced play out in our small groups.

Realistic small groups. Realistic Christianity begins with what is and then asks what's possible within the confines of what is. Instead of starting with God's dream to redeem all things, we start with the realities we face in life. Since we are busy, overwhelmed and underresourced, we look at how we can lead groups in a way that does not infringe too much on group members. We lower expectations to something like "attend the meeting." We might say we want more, that we are committed to loving one another and the world, but deep down we know that the way we do life precludes us from doing more than paying lip service to the idea of living in community and entering God's mission. So we make the best of it.

Radical small groups. Then there are those who embrace radical Christianity, often as a reaction against those who live realistically. With these group leaders there is no room for compromise. They call Christians to step out and go above and beyond, to sacrifice to extremes. Activism, mission and outreach consume small groups that take this approach. Zealous progress toward passionate Christianity and getting something done for the kingdom is the focus. They attack the world with a vengeance, seeking to do what Jesus has told them to do. But here's the thing: the focus too often lies so much on the action or the mission that these groups end up doing violence to others and themselves. They rally around the cause, but in doing so they miss the way of Jesus.

Enclave small groups. Too many groups have been entrapped by this way as they seek to escape from life in order to do religious stuff. While they talk about how God is alive, what they do inside the group has little to do with life outside the group. Hope lies in the religious activity, not in the life of God at work in our world. The most common form of the enclave is called "Bible study." We get together to talk about the information of the Bible and learn some very good facts about the Bible. And this might have some impact on our personal spirituality. But the goal is processing biblical information. Others are welcome, but they must come and be like us if they want to get to know Jesus.

Idealistic small groups. Idealism causes us to find the "right" way of doing church and small groups. We assume that if we unlock this right way, we will unlock the life of God in our midst. Usually this involves arguments about the way the early church operated and how to follow that biblical approach. Here's the problem: through the years there have been so many "right" interpretations of the way New Testament house churches operated that any claim to rightness can be countered endlessly. We just don't have enough detailed explanation about first-century house churches to define an ideal New Testament model. Even if we did, our focus would shift away from the way of Jesus as we tried to figure out the "right" methodology for implementation.

The way of Jesus offers small groups an alternative paradigm. This way calls us into the "the creation of a distinct community with its own deviant set of values and its coherent way of incarnating them."[3] We don't need more groups that convene average American Christians to help them keep doing what they're already doing. We don't need nice groups that allow us to live in our normal American patterns while nothing distinctive or "deviant" stands in contrast to the surrounding culture. We need groups that will live in love and stand in contrast to what we know. John Howard Yoder wrote, "The church is God's people gathered as a unit, as a people, gathered to do business in His name, to find what it means here and now to put into practice this different quality of life which is God's promise to them and to the world and their promise to God and service to the world."[4]

BREAKING OUT OF WHAT WE HEAR

I've led groups in all four modes listed above, and they all—each differently, of course—confine us to repeating what we already know. We develop a vision for real community. We study the Bible and see how God has called us to make a difference. We add community and mission to our established paradigms and continue to get what we have long gotten in our small groups.

What does it take then to break out of the paradigms that control what we hear? Is more training what we need? Will more sermons or teaching on the topic change things? How about another book?

Yes, yes and yes! We need all kinds of proclamations that call out of the normal and present the vision for the way of Jesus. But if we're leading a small group, we need something slightly different. Proclamations might open the door, but they won't necessarily change our paradigm so that we develop eyes to see and ears to hear. For that, leaders need ways to ask questions and foster conversations. When we ask good questions, we provide opportunities for people to discover for themselves the radical nature of the kingdom of God. For instance:

- How does the kingdom contrast with the ways of the world, especially in Western cultures?
- What does it mean to love God when the world is pulling us in ways that are unloving?
- How do things like workaholism, our addiction to power, our need for entertainment and other common patterns hinder the kingdom?

In what follows, I offer some questions around three rhythms of group life that form us in the way of Jesus. These three questions have at their center the Great Commandment (Matthew 22:37) and the Great Commission (Matthew 28:19-20). I explain them in greater depth in my book *Missional Small Groups: Becoming a Community that Makes a Difference in the World*[5] and the study guide. We can adopt these three rhythms as small groups in order to participate in what God is doing to form us into people of the kingdom way:

1. ***Communion with God.*** The Great Commandment reads, "Love the Lord your God with all your heart and with all your soul and with all your mind. This is the first and greatest commandment" (Matthew 22:37-38).

2. ***Relating well to one another.*** Jesus named the second commandment when he said, "And the second is like it: 'Love your neighbor as yourself'" (Matthew 22:39). In the first epistle by John, we read that "Whoever claims to love God yet hates a brother or sister is a liar" (1 John 4:20).

3. ***Engagement with our world.*** We are to engage the world by being a people of witness. The first part of the Great Commission reads, "Go into the world." Jesus also told the disciples, "But you will receive power when the Holy Spirit comes on you; and you will be my witnesses in Jerusalem, and in all Judea and Samaria, and to the ends of the earth" (Acts 1:8).

These three rhythms work together to call us into the way of Jesus—as illustrated by the diagram below.

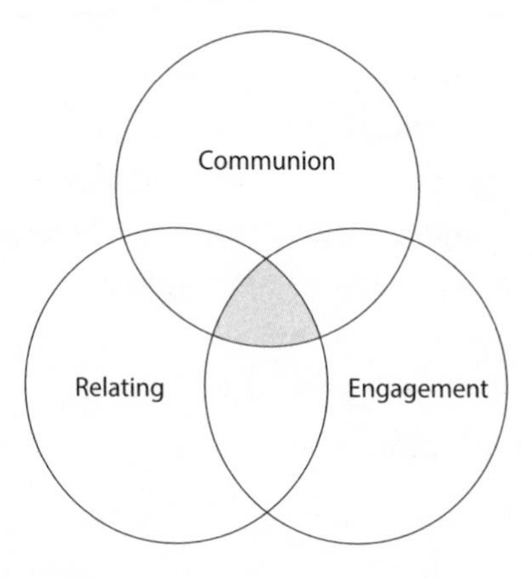

Figure 3.1. Three rhythms of group life

Discipleship or spiritual information is the dynamic found in the Great Commission: "Therefore go and make disciples of all nations, baptizing them in the name of the Father and of the Son and of the Holy Spirit, and teaching them to obey everything I have commanded you. And surely I am with you always, to the very end of the age" (Matthew 28:19-20). Basically, this is about growing in the three dynamics listed above.

As we ask and answer questions about these rhythms of the way of Jesus, we will find ourselves advancing along that way. In what follows I introduce questions for each rhythm. These questions are derived from those who've written about group life from a variety of traditions. The goal is to generate conversations from different angles so we might hear things differently. You may not be familiar with these writers or their way of talking about group life, but that's the point. If we want to see things differently, we have to ask different questions.

THE QUESTIONS OF COMMUNION

People long to belong somewhere. We are created with an inner wiring to connect to each other. It's part of the DNA of being human. However, a leader cannot force this belonging to take place. A leader can talk about the reality of how we are wired to connect, but connections cannot be mandated. If leaders try to prescribe exactly how group members will experience belonging, they actually foster and reinforce loneliness. Why? Because members are compelled to interact with one another directly. They relate in a way that puts pressure on others to fill their emptiness, to be for them what they have not been able to be in and of themselves. Henri Nouwen puts it this way:

> Friendship and love cannot develop in the form of anxious clinging to each other. . . . As long as our loneliness brings us together with the hope that together we no longer will be

> alone, we castigate each other with our unfulfilled and unrealistic desires for oneness, inner tranquility and uninterrupted experience of communion.[6]

Leading with predetermined answers instead of questions propagates this clinging because individuals try to connect without actually examining their loneliness. They just do small groups the way they're supposed to do, as outlined by the book or by the pastor. Isolated people try to fix their isolation by clinging to others. Even those who seem strong and independent connect to others in order to get their needs met. We cling like hungry leeches, assuming that this is the way we'll find belonging.

The alternative to relating directly is to relate to one another in the "space between." That is the space where Christ exists. The most direct path to ministry is communion with Christ. The only way to relate well is to cling to Christ, the one who lives in the space between us. Nouwen writes:

> Friendship and community are, first of all, inner qualities allowing human togetherness to be the playful expression of a much larger reality. They can never be claimed, planned or organized, but in our innermost self the place can be formed where they can be received as gifts.[7]

We are connected not as individuals who cling together like melded metals but as individuals who are in Christ, and Christ is in us who are joined together for a journey. The Christ in me is united with the Christ in you. And the Christ in us draws us together. This is not about clinging but mutual identity in Christ.

To find Christ in the space between, we have to learn to ask questions like:

- Where is the deep loneliness within me?
- How do I tend to cling to others to fix my loneliness?

- What does it look like for me to find myself in Christ?
- How can I share this struggle to find myself in Christ with others in my group?

THE QUESTIONS OF RELATING

In Western society, we have lost the sense of family. We no longer think in terms of putting down roots. Friendships are expendable. When we try to connect with others, we often ask questions like, "What's in this for me?" or "How can this benefit my life?" or "What's this going to cost me?"

It's easy to talk about the problem of individualism. It's a lot harder to talk about my own individualism. The normal approach to small groups is for people to jump in and "make friends," but in most cases this results in a gathering of disparate parts. We have groups of individualists who are trying to connect on a regular basis, but they are not relating in a way that expresses the life of unity. It's almost as if we are trying to join individualism with community and hold on to both at the same time, an act of futility. Individualism is based on a certain set of life practices that stand in contradiction to the practices of community, and it keeps groups mired in mediocrity. Putting a group of individualists in the same room for a meeting once a week is a good start, but it's not something for which we should settle.

We need questions that help us discover a new way of relating, questions that cause us to see that we're more than the sum of our individual parts. The Russian Orthodox pastor Seraphim Sigrist was shaped by an underground church during Soviet reign. He writes, "Community life is a journey toward, and an entering into, a space that is immensely greater than the combination of all personal spaces, and into a life that is far more than that of all our separate lives taken together."[8]

This is a new space where who we are as a group is far more than what we add up to be as group members. Here the "I" is grounded in "we." In other words, who I am is shaped by who we are together. And in this sense, I become far more in the midst of this "we" than "I" am when I'm trying to hold on to my individualism.

This does not mean we give up our individuality. Instead our individuality flourishes when we experience life together. Russian theologians have used the word *sobornost* to describe this. This word is hard to translate into English. It includes the idea of being united but goes beyond our typical ways of talking about unity. While it involves a sense of shared vision and beliefs, it has more to do with sharing a life that lines up with the vision and beliefs. Sigrist writes that at the heart of *sobornost* is "sharing life together without any loss of your true self; we are no longer isolated from each other and no longer isolated from the whole of God's creation."[9] We become our true selves while at the same time become more than ourselves. How's that for a paradox?

Questions that might open the path to finding the "I" in the "we" include:

- How do I tend to use others for my own personal benefit?
- How have I viewed this group as a good for my own consumption?
- What would have to change in order for us to experience the group as more than the sum of its parts?
- How could this group serve to shape my individual identity?

THE QUESTIONS OF ENGAGEMENT

In *Life Together*, Dietrich Bonhoeffer's masterpiece on Christian community, he opens with words about mission:

> Jesus Christ lived in the midst of his enemies. In the end all

> his disciples abandoned him. On the cross he was all alone, surrounded by criminals and the jeering crowds. He had come for the express purpose of bringing peace to the enemies of God. So Christians, too, belong not in the seclusion of a cloistered life but in the midst of enemies. There they find their mission, their work.[10]

Life together is diasporatic community, not cloistered community. *Diaspora* is the Greek word used to describe the scattered nature of God's people throughout the world. And it implies that Christian community is about living in a way that engages the world around us. Bonhoeffer continues:

> According to God's will, the Christian church is a scattered people, scattered like seed "to all the kingdoms of the earth" (Deut. 28:25). That is the curse and the promise. God's people must live in distant lands among unbelievers, but they will be the seed of the kingdom of God in all the world.[11]

God's kind of community does not happen in an enclave or as an exclusive club. God's kind of community happens in the midst of life, right in front of those who don't understand why we worship and love the way we do. What does this look like in the local contexts where our groups gather? The answer to this question is the reason that engagement cannot be prescribed. There is no one-size-fits-all way to do this. Every local situation requires different ways of engaging. Some key questions to ask might include:

- What does it mean to do community in such a way that the world can see it?
- How have our previous experiences in community been an enclave?
- How might our group be on mission together?
- How can our individual missions expand if we work together?

THE QUESTIONS OF DISCIPLESHIP

Simply stated, discipleship is just showing others how to commune with God, relate to one another and engage with neighbors and networks. This is all a gift. Discipleship is the work of the Spirit in us. God is the one forming us. Discipleship manifests as we participate in this gift of communion, loving each other and engaging the world. However, too often we make discipleship about our efforts. We put ourselves at the center of "spiritual" formation. This can be illustrated by the command to "make disciples" (Matthew 18:19-20).

On one level, we make disciples in that we choose to invest in people who need spiritual direction and guidance. However, on another level we don't actually "make" disciples, at least not in the way we think of when we use the word "make." In English, the definition of this word involves the creation of an inanimate object. We make computers. We make houses. We make model airplanes. I don't find the word "make" very useful when it comes to helping other people love God, love each other and engage their neighbors with the gospel. We use the word "make" in a prescriptive way. We make something that is predetermined. When we do this, we become the active agents of "discipleship," where we are trying to produce something for God. The words of Jean Vanier are helpful here:

> Workers come together in a factory to produce things and to make a good living wage. Soldiers come together in an army to prepare for war. People come together in a community because they want to create a place of caring. Community is not for producing things outside of itself; it is not a gathering of people struggling to win a cause. It is a place of communion where people care for others, and are cared for by others; a place where they become vulnerable to one another.[12]

We do not "make" disciples. We are formed as disciples in community together as the Spirit works in us. Discipleship is about people, and people cannot be controlled or predetermined. We cannot prescribe the path of discipleship. Instead, discipleship occurs as we spend time together so that one person discovers from another where he falls short so he can die and rise to new life. Discipleship is about demonstration more than it is about instruction. It is not about going out and forming people into what we think they need to be based on what we see on the surface.

The practical way of discipleship is about spiritual formation—that is, formation by and through the Spirit, not by and through the another person who is the "discipler." The Spirit is forming a redemptive society that's involved in making all things new. We are being formed by the Spirit to participate in this relational adventure that manifests God's body on earth. The great Quaker theologian and philosopher Elton Trueblood wrote, "If [you] want to make a difference, here in a clear way, make all within your society members of the crew and permit no passengers."[13] We must tap into the way the Spirit is making and forming us into a society of the Jesus way.

The questions might look like this:

- What is God doing in me?
- What is God doing in us?
- What is God doing around us?
- What does God want to do through us?

PRACTICAL TIP: FOCUS ON THOSE WITH EYES TO SEE

We cannot force people to enter into the way of Jesus. Many of them may agree with the vision, but that doesn't mean they actually "hear" it. This is where the questions are so important. Listen to how people respond. Who is already asking questions like these? Who is expressing frustration with the status quo? Who wants to talk about distinct ways of following Jesus? Who is willing to put some extra thought and time into answering the questions?

The goal is to work with people who already have a sense of urgency to experience a different kind of group life. One way to determine this is to lead people through a short-term experience that introduces the ideas found in this book. (My book *Difference Makers* is designed to do this.) As people go through such introductory experiences, I've observed four typical responses.

First are those who want a small group meeting every week and that's all; they don't really want to experience life with others. They scoff at the idea of sharing regular meals, watching one another's kids or going on vacation together. They would rather have a broad range of surface-level friends instead of a primary group with whom they share life deeply. Or maybe they're content with Bible study alone.

When we encounter such people, I've found it best to just let them have their point of view. It takes a lot of effort to introduce them to a new idea. Most likely they fall into the late adopter category, which means they'll take a while to come around to a new perspective—but often they eventually do.

The second group includes people who are attracted to the way of Jesus but the realities of work schedules, family life and other commitments make it unrealistic to jump into life together. The idea is compelling. The know they want it. But life habits preclude them from doing it well. Such people usually have to take their busyness to the cross and examine what they're willing to invest their lives in. Trying to add the way of Jesus on top of everything else is a recipe for mediocrity. Often these people are some of the most committed in the church, but they must recognize the temptation of doing one more thing. Those who catch the vision for the way of Jesus and are willing to make changes—that is, go to the cross—are ready for the next level.

The third group comprises people who desire the way of Jesus but need significant development in their relationship skills. Many of us in North America have been formed by relationship patterns that undermine group life on the way of Jesus. For instance, we've lost the ability to waste time with one another and eat together (see chapter seven). Or maybe we need to learn how to experience conflict in healthy ways (see chapter nine). In many cases, we just need to learn to develop some basic skills of how to greet one another, how to listen to each other, and how to go deeper with a small group of friends instead of having tons of paper-thin acquaintances.

A fourth group is made up of those who are ready and able to enter into the relational way of Jesus. They have a sense of urgency and a desire for more. For these people, provide an introductory experience that initiates them into the way of Jesus. There are quite a few resources that are now available that do this very thing.[14] Find a tool that fits your context and tradition and lead people to the cross. Help those who have eyes to see process practical ways of moving into the ways of the kingdom as a community.

YOUR SMALL GROUP JOURNEY

While there are many great strategies and ideas for how your group can move forward on the journey into communion, relating, engagement and discipleship, the key is to start with the questions. These questions are meant to drive you to your knees so you can hear what the Spirit is saying. This opens doors for experimenting with how to live out of these questions. Practical ideas can be implemented as God provides direction on how he is calling your group into the kingdom way.

As you ask and answer these questions, you will find that these rhythms are not four disparate songs that play one at a time. Each affects the other three. As you grow in one, the rhythms converge into one melody.

The way we pray affects our discipleship, which affects our ability to reach out and engage our neighbors. When we love non-Christians and invest in their lives, we find that we have to depend on one another more and we grow in our relationships. This is the way of walking with Jesus—living out here and now the self-sacrificial love of the cross. In turn, this increases our encounter with the presence of God, which leads us to the second practice.

four

Gather in the Presence

The Second Practice

I have a confession to make. I kinda like "chick flicks." Not because I'm trying to score points with my wife, but because I enjoy a good love story. Now, of course, far too many are so predictable that the outcome is clear from the opening scene. I prefer those where love is expressed in the midst of a sudden twist or an unexpected serendipity. From the line "You had me at 'hello'" from *Jerry Maguire* to the story of a courtship read by an elderly man to his Alzheimer's-stricken wife in *The Notebook* to the unusual relationship between C. S. Lewis and Joy Davidson depicted in *Shadowlands*, there is something truthful about the experience of love in the midst of the unexpected twists and turns of life.

Love, whether in romance or in friendship, is an unexpected revelation. It's not something we can predict, control or cajole. We choose to love and we choose to receive love, but the experience of love is a surprising, out-of-the-blue blessing. Love sneaks over the walls we've put up to protect ourselves and gently whispers, "I am with you, and I'm not going anywhere." This kind of love, while not plastered on billboards or broadcast across airwaves, wakes us from the slumber of predictable normalcy. This unexpected being with the other—whether friend or spouse—startles us out of average.

Love and presence are two sides of the same coin. And this is true of God also. The Gospel of Matthew closes with Jesus' words: "And surely I am with you always, to the very end of the age" (Matthew 28:20). The presence of Jesus is always with us, and because "God is love" (1 John 4:8), the love of God is always with us. Leading groups in the way of Jesus presumes that Jesus is on the journey with us. We are not doing this without him. And I would propose that God's presence—and his love—are most evident in the unpredictable moments we experience in the valleys and on the mountaintops (Psalm 23).

Too many times, though, we do group meetings in a way that tries to even out the ups and downs to a level plain. Over the years I've asked many small groups leaders the question, "How did your group meeting go this week?" The most common answer goes something like this: "It was good. We had a good discussion about the lesson. And we ended in prayer." In other words, the group followed the plan as outlined by the lesson. It went as expected—an average group meeting.

If a group stays focused on the study guide or Bible lesson for the entire meeting and does everything according to plan, then we must ask, "Where was God?" Of course, God was (and is always) there, but what happened that was unexpected? Was there deviation from the plan—a person who disrupted the meeting, discussion about one question for the entire night, a member sharing a deep need, or twenty minutes of laughter from the sharing of life stories? When such detours from the plan occur, we should ask how God is showing up through the deviation.

When we ignore or gloss over the unexpected—or, worse yet, when nothing unexpected ever happens—we miss the opportunity to encounter the presence of Jesus. The unexpected creates space for us to see the kingdom. It pulls us into what makes us distinctively God's—the presence of God and the experience of his love. Without God's presence we're just a religious club talking about the facts of the Bible or a group of people taking on a cause. With his presence we embark on a journey of serendipitous love.

MEETING AS IF GOD DIDN'T EXIST

Many of us have too frequently led groups as if God did not exist. We have our plan, usually in the form of a Bible study or a vision for mission. Then we attack it, assuming that our plan is clearly dictated by the Bible. Yet we move forward without any sense of dependence on God's Spirit.

This reality should not surprise us. I've found it quite easy to go through the daily stuff of life with a totally secular point of view. It's the reality of the world we live in. It's the air we breathe. Ours is a scientific age, a logical world that can explain everything. And if we cannot explain it, all we need to do is get more information. Eventually we'll understand why everything works the way it does.

This is often referred to as a "disenchanted" world. Before the events of the last three hundred years, it was unheard of in the West to walk through a day as if there were no God. The world was full of mysteries that could not be explained. Now we know everything. And if we don't know it, we Google it on our smartphones. Enchantment is gone. Mystery, wonder and the presence of otherness are distant memories. And because God is beyond our control and full of life that cannot be fully explained, it's hard to see how he fits into our world.[1]

We cannot go back to a pre-disenchantment state. We are shaped by disenchantment whether we like it or not. Common life operates as if God did not exist. So we go to church and attend our small groups to talk about God, but then we return to our daily lives and go about the status quo. We know that God exists, but we're not quite sure how he intersects our world today.

I am convinced that we've become so accustomed to disenchanted leadership that we don't ever recognize it. We know how to study the Bible and are skilled at talking about Jesus' life and ministry. We have plenty of experience with good group discussions. And technology lets us pipe in the best Bible teaching in the world via DVD or YouTube. The result? We spend far more time talking about Jesus than we do encountering his presence. We know God's story, but how much do we tell the story with our life together?

On top of this, small groups are focusing more and more on the tangible mission of God, which often turns into activism. The group attains a clear vision for mission and puts great effort into doing something like serving the poor or reaching the lost. And since the Bible places great emphasis on both, the group feels it has a strong foundation for its work. It's just simple obedience. But we can go forth in mission without any expectation that God is present with us.

As soon as I lead in such a way that I assume I know how a group should work, I'm most likely missing the way God wants to show up in my group. But when we experience the presence of Jesus in our groups, we shift from a mindset of studying the stories of God to actually embodying those stories. The story becomes our story as we live into it and it enters into us. We shift from making plans for what we'll do for God to serving others at cost to ourselves because the love of Jesus flows out of us in concrete ways. The difference is subtle but significant. The actions might look the same, but when there is no presence, we become the center of the action. With the presence, Jesus is the center, the lead actor in our group.

IN THE NAME OF JESUS

Jesus told us, "For where two or three gather in my name, there am I with them" (Matthew 18:20). What a promise! The presence of Jesus changes people's lives, heals people of sin, unites broken relationships and sets people on a rock. What exactly is the presence of

Jesus? What does it mean to meet in Jesus' name? Where is Jesus?

If we are going to be a people of presence, we must begin by asking where Jesus is already present. Rather than doing our group activities and asking God in prayer to bless what we just did, we begin by acknowledging that God is already present in our midst when we gather. We simply confess aloud that Jesus is alive and present, thanking him for this reality.

Presence is what drives communion, relating and engagement. We cannot assume that we can make these things happen or that we can just mimic what Jesus or other heroes of the faith have done. The life that Jesus wants to see happen in our groups depends upon Christ. It all flows from him.

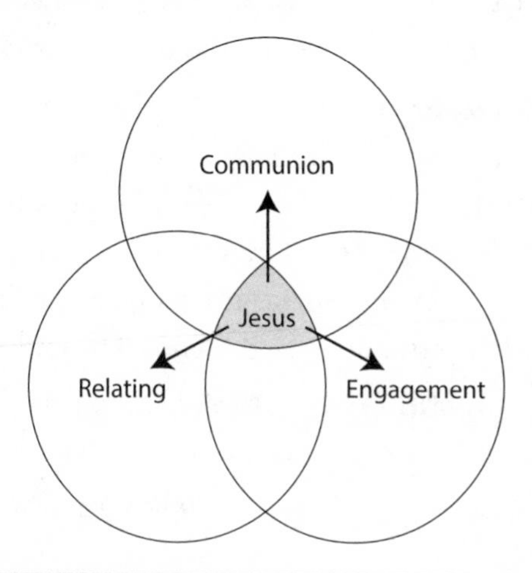

Figure 4.1. The presence of Jesus

When we recognize this, we can facilitate meetings and share informal time together in such a way that recognizes this reality and promotes it. We don't have to make the presence of Jesus happen. We welcome Jesus. We make space for his life in our midst. The question is: How do we do this?

We have lots of creative curricula at our disposal that help us connect people in group discussion. The best focus on open-ended questions that get people talking about a specific Bible passage in a way that moves from understanding to implementation. The key is for the group leader or designated facilitator to refrain from doing all the talking or preaching a message to the group. The small group is not a miniature version of the Sunday congregation or a Sunday school class receiving the teacher's instruction. Effective small groups develop in the context of conversations, not monologues.

In most cases, we can shape our open-ended conversations with three types of questions:

- ***Observation questions.*** These questions lead to conversations about what the passage says. For instance, a common observation question is, "What stands out to you from the passage?"
- ***Interpretation questions.*** In this category we find questions that get to the meaning of the passage. These might include, "What did Jesus mean when he said . . . ?" Or "Who was the audience Jesus was addressing?" Sometimes we might present a little background information to help the group understand the point. But never is the conversation to be dominated by interpretive data.
- ***Application questions.*** The last couple of questions should focus on what the passage means for our lives. Here we might ask, "What has God been saying to us specifically during the discussion?"

These three types of questions can be easily written up before a meeting so that the leader has four or five questions to guide the conversation. However, I can safely say that I have never led a meeting I would call "good," much less "great," that has followed the exact path dictated by the questions on my sheet of paper. The questions got me started, but the conversations created space for the unexpected.

As I stated earlier, if at the end of a meeting we have followed the plan of the printed curriculum exactly, then we have probably missed God. He does not conform to our curriculum. The curriculum is meant to get us started so we can get to more important questions that stir unexpected conversations.

When I lead a group with a printed curriculum, I'm listening for responses that might reveal where God is at work beneath the surface. I'm listening for how people are subtly, and usually unconsciously, responding to deeper questions that deal with the three big arenas of life. These questions are:

Who am I? If you want to see what God is doing in others, listen to how people perceive themselves. Personal identity is crucial to our walk with God and as people open up in groups, their stories will come out. Their histories and how those histories have influenced who they are have shaped their journeys with Jesus. As people are free to explore what God is saying to them personally, they'll start asking related questions like "Who are we?" "Who is God?" "What does that have to do with me and our life as a group?"

Where do I belong? Most people today have little sense of connection with others. But as they begin to experience a sense of belonging within the group, they begin to ask things like "Who is my spiritual family?" "What does this family look like under God's direction?" "How can I invest in this family so that it can be what God wants it to be?"

What can I offer this world? Within all of us there is a need to offer our lives to something greater than ourselves. Often we ask this question out of self-centeredness—we want to be needed. But as we become grounded in Christ's love, our questions begin to shift. We begin to ask, "What can we do today to bring beauty into the ugliness of this world?" "What is God asking me and us to do right now?" "What gifts do we have to offer the world?" "What are the needs around us that God is calling us to meet?"

These three big life questions loosely relate to the three rhythms found in the last chapter. We find who we are in Communion. We discover where we belong through Relating. And we explore what we can offer the world through Engagement. In the midst of this, Christ is at work and is present at the center of it all.

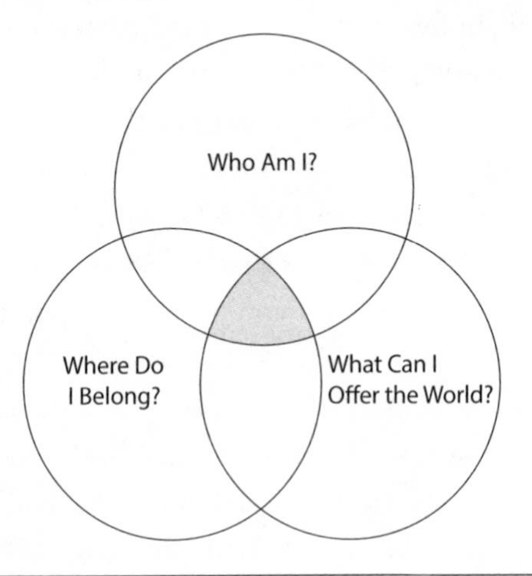

Figure 4.2. Life questions

As you encounter the presence of Jesus, you will be asking life questions about the next steps of the journey that incorporate all three of the above questions. Groups must ask questions regarding "What's our next step on the journey of the way of Jesus?" When we first start asking this question as immature Christians, the focus is on me and my journey. But as we grow up, we begin to see that discipleship and spiritual formation are not about me but the fact that God is forming us into a community of maturity and mission. We begin to ask, "What is God calling this group to do differently?" "How can we be prepared for that next leg?"

At times you as the leader might ask these questions of the group directly, but for the most part they're best used to shape the way you listen so you can hear what people are really saying. All of us are asking these questions at some level. The challenge is to face the barriers in our lives that keep us from answering these questions well. And many times, all people need is someone who will take the time to go beyond the obvious responses to hear what's really going on.

These three big life questions can be further developed so as to shape conversations in the group meetings and outside of them. Some questions might include:

- Where am I seeing Jesus at work this week?
- What is Jesus showing us in his Word?
- How can we see Jesus at work among our group today?
- How am I enjoying people around me this week?
- Who is Jesus drawing my attention toward?
- How can I simplify life to make space to enjoy others?
- How can I take a step to join Jesus in doing good?
- What vulnerability or needs has God shown me this week?
- Where have I held back from doing good because of the potential cost?
- What is Jesus drawing my attention toward within me?
- How do I see God forming me to become like Jesus?
- Where do I have joy about what Jesus is doing, and where do I have discomfort?
- How can we grow in walking alongside each other?
- What would I like the group to ask me about next week?
- How are we uniquely formed to contribute to each other?[2]

PRACTICAL TIPS THAT FOSTER THE PRESENCE OF JESUS

There are quite a few techniques that help create space for the presence of Jesus. They include the following:

Meet weekly. The statistics are conclusive. Jim Egli has performed extensive research on this topic and writes about it in his book *Small Groups, Big Impact*. Groups that gather weekly have greater spiritual vitality and are much more likely to affect others outside the group than groups meeting less frequently. If a group meets only twice per month, it will fall short. While there might be some exceptions, this is a basic rule.[3]

Welcome people as they arrive. This might sound rudimentary. You might think that since everyone knows everyone and all are comfortable with one another, it's not important to greet people as they arrive. But when we assume this, we miss the opportunity to greet one another with affection. We are not especially good at this in the Western world, but in places like Russia, those who know each other the best greet each other with the most passion.

Share communion together. It's difficult to provide practical instructions here since there are so many different traditions related to communion. My suggestion is to simply practice communion in your group in a way that honors your tradition.

Manage the space. Make sure the temperature is set right. Put away the dog. Set the atmosphere with a candle. Take care of distracting smells. Make sure the electronics—if you're using them—are working right. It's remarkable how the small things can take a group meeting to the next level. Make sure people are sitting in a circle or at least an oval. The goal is for everyone to have a clear line of sight to all other members. Shy people often pull their chairs back a few inches to hide a bit, while outgoing people will pull forward. Encourage people to keep to the circle so that everyone can see everyone else.

Explain, explain and explain again. Help those who are new understand what you're doing. Don't leave them in the dark. If you sing during worship, make sure everyone has access to the words. If you're talking about the Bible or referring to your pastor's recent message, don't assume everyone knows what you're talking about. Avoid big theological words. There better be a good reason for saying things like "We are justified by the blood of the lamb" or "We live in an eschatological age." If you do say such things, please explain what you mean for the rest of us.

Facilitate conversations. If the leader is talking more than fifty percent of the time, the group is missing out on dialogue. This takes us back to the leader's role in asking good questions that relate to the big questions of life. When we are asking life questions, people are much more likely to share and open their souls to one another.

End on time. Even if people want to remain and talk or even have extended times of prayer, give permission for people to leave if they need to. This is especially important for those who are newer participants in the group. Having an official ending time creates a safer environment.

These techniques help prepare the way for a group to engage Christ's presence. The rest of the chapter focuses on discovery and adaptive actions that take it to the next level.

LISTENING FOSTERS PRESENCE

The degree to which we listen to each other will be the degree to which we experience the presence of Jesus in our midst. To listen to the other requires that we refrain from some common habits that hinder our ability to let the other speak. These usually come in the following forms:

Judging another person as they share. As people open up, it's easy to jump to conclusions about their actions or motivations.

Comparing another person's story to your own experience. When people open up and share, they don't want to hear how other people experienced something similar. That only discounts their experience.

Fixing, advising, saving or setting straight. When people reveal their souls, they are not asking to be fixed or counseled on how they can get over their problem. They are asking to be heard and embraced in the midst of the reality they are facing.

Instead of judging, comparing or fixing, we need to allow people to reveal who they are. This creates space for the presence of God since God is always relating to us as we truly are. The practice of listening is first an attitude of the heart—we listen from the inside out—however, there are a few visible ways we can express that we're truly listening.

Give space for silence. Many times the tone of a meeting will shift to one of stillness and quiet. Protect this time and guide the group to listen and reflect. When we allow brief breaks after someone shares instead of filling the air with talk, we give room for people to express deeper things that are often kept within. At times, the best way to honor one another is to give space for silence by guiding the group to listen to what's going on in their hearts.

Respond with additional questions. These questions can fall into the following groups:[4]

Clarifying the issue. These questions help people name the real issues they're facing. They might include:

- "You said . . . What did you mean by that?"
- "Could you identify your concern or challenge in one sentence?"

Clarifying the context. Sometimes autobiographical information helps others understand the nature of what is being shared. You might ask:

- "What has occurred that caused you to see things this way?"
- "Is this related to [an issue shared in the past]?"

Clarifying the direction. These kinds of questions help identify what God is doing in the midst of the situation:

- "What do you sense God saying to you as you share?"
- "How does God want to meet you in the midst of this situation?"

Offer encouragement. This is crucial when someone shares something that lies deep within their heart. A gentle tone of voice and repetition of what's been shared are important. For example: "Jim, I hear you saying that you've never been able to forgive your father for the cruel way he treated you." Edification means that I hear your need, then I hear Christ's voice, then I share what he has given to me to say so that you may be built up.

EATING TOGETHER FOSTERS PRESENCE

When I ask the question "Where was Jesus?" while reading the Gospels, I'm continually shocked by how often he was found eating. Food and Jesus come together. We see Jesus relaxing with his disciples over meals, teaching them over dinner and even using parables about food. We see him engaging neighbors and networks during meals and parties. A primary example is the party at Matthew's house at which tax collectors and sinners had assembled. We also have evidence that the early church met most frequently over shared meals. And we know that worship occurred with the celebration of communion.

There's something about food that moves us beyond technical solutions to deeper engagement with the problems we encounter in our small groups. Some issues are better addressed over the dinner table than in a strategy session or planning meeting. When we share a meal, something adaptive occurs, something creative that we cannot fully explain. We enter a space where we accept one another and meet with God in a way we cannot control. Sharing meals and experiencing the presence coincide more than any of us might expect.

After all, the final coming of the kingdom in its full manifestation is described as a great banquet (see Luke 14). Sharing meals now is a foretaste of what is to come. Meaningful conversations take place over a common meal where people sit with one another and talk. Answers to adaptive challenges arise as we wait in God's presence over the communion meal. And we discover new ways God wants to work through us as we eat with our neighbors who are not formally part of the group.

Food puts something between us that creates space for Christ to be in our midst. It teaches us to relate to one another through Christ. This is especially true when the communion meal is practiced. Food invites mystery. It makes space for the fact that I cannot relate to you directly and make an object out of you. In this space, I learn to relate to you as a person through the presence of Christ.

CHILDREN FOSTER PRESENCE

One of the most common questions I've gotten through the years has been what to do with the children during a meeting. Almost always, the question comes with the expectation that I will provide a technical answer to a technical problem, that I will provide a list of specific solutions that allow the adults to get back to the "real" meeting and have a good discussion. After I provide a few ideas, they go back and try to implement them. But nothing changes. The kids remain a distraction.

Children are not the barrier keeping our groups from God's presence. Most often our attitude about the children reveals our attitude about God's presence. Jesus said, "Let the little children come to me" (Matthew 19:14), but most of the time in our church life we send the children off to another room. Jesus also said that unless we have the same attitude as a child, there is not a place for us in God's kingdom (Matthew 18:3). The presence of children can clear a path for the presence of Jesus.

While there are practical things we can do to organize the children in a small group, the most important thing to do is this: treat them as full participants in the life of the group. They are not future members of the community. They are full members. If our attitudes do not reflect this, it does not matter what kind of children's activity we set up. Children know when adults are (or are not) pursuing the way of Jesus.

In practical terms, this means that children should be welcomed and affirmed just like every adult who is part of the group. Include them in the icebreaker, the meal time and worship. Then adults can take turns with the kids each week doing some kind of activity or lesson. Maybe it's just going to a park or having fun together. There are many options. The main point is to embrace the children and let them participate. They may very well be the voice of God in your midst.

AN EXERCISE THAT FOSTERS PRESENCE

In Colossians, Paul instructs us in some actions that create space for the presence of Jesus in the midst of group meetings. The passage reads:

> Therefore, as God's chosen people, holy and dearly loved, clothe yourselves with compassion, kindness, humility, gentleness and patience. Bear with each other and forgive one another if any of you has a grievance against someone. Forgive as the Lord forgave you. And over all these virtues put on love, which binds them all together in perfect unity.
>
> Let the peace of Christ rule in your hearts, since as members of one body you were called to peace. And be thankful. Let the message of Christ dwell among you richly as you teach and admonish one another with all wisdom through psalms, hymns, and songs from the Spirit, singing to God with gratitude in your hearts. (Colossians 3:12-16)

Notice that this passage is written to a group of people. We cannot have compassion, kindness, humility, gentleness and patience while isolated. Through the years I've experimented with an activity that always ends up with unexpected blessings and doors opened to the presence of Jesus in the midst of a group. I've found it to be especially helpful when a group is caught in a rut and needs to break out. Here's how to instruct the group:

Step one. Over the next few days, seek an encounter with God by yourself in a way that's meaningful to you. Break the normal pattern of praying. Go for a walk and talk to God as you experience nature. Listen to a CD while you drive and worship God. Read a devotional book and write a journal entry. Find a painting online of Jesus on the cross and look at it while you pray and thank God for your salvation.

Step two. This experience with God can serve as your contribution to the group. If you connected with God in a song, bring the CD and play it. If you read something in a book that spoke to you, read it aloud and share why it had meaning for you. Maybe you went for a walk and picked up a rock along the way. Bring that rock and share what you experienced on your walk. If you wrote in your journal, share an entry. If you painted something, show it. If you were touched by a poem, read it. If you saw a movie that touched you, play a clip. You need not be profound or deep. The point is to share your experience with God with others.

These insights will feed the group's prayers, and it will connect members with each other more closely. Our vulnerability always speaks. By simply sharing our connection with God, we build one another up and experience what Paul wrote about. Here are some basic guidelines:

- When you meet, there is no Bible study per se. This is an invitation for people to share what they have to offer.
- Read Colossians 3:12-16. Someone should state that this is a time to practice this passage, not to study it.
- Open the floor for people to share voluntarily what they have brought to the group.
- Commit as a group to listening to what each person offers. For some, this is a very vulnerable experience. Affirmation is crucial.

- This is not a time of preaching or instructing—the focus of the sharing should come out of each individual's encounter with God. If someone goes down a didactic track, steer him or her in a different direction.
- Emphasize that whatever is shared should have an encouraging tone. This is about experiencing the love of God, not about religious performance or self-condemnation. If someone shares a condemning experience with the group, listen, but also help that person to hear God's love.

EMBRACE THE UNEXPECTED

Years ago I was in conversation with a friend who had been hurt by a legalistic experience in the church. He was sharing his story (which relates to "Who am I?") and was trying to navigate life now that he was no longer in that kind of a church (which connects to "Where do I belong?"). While we were sitting there, it became obvious that he was carrying quite a bit of bitterness and needed to release those people who had hurt him. He realized that if he wanted to move forward with God, he had to take steps to forgive those people ("What's next?").

Because I cared about the questions my friend was raising, I gave him room to explore what was going on in his life. I did not preach. I did not quote Scripture. I listened. I asked questions. I tried to create an atmosphere where the Spirit could reveal what was going on.

I have also been in group meetings that don't do this. We read a Scripture on a topic like forgiveness. Someone teaches on what forgiveness is and is not. We talk about what the pastor said in the sermon about forgiveness. Then people quote other Scriptures about the importance of forgiveness and what happened in the Bible when people did not forgive. Then the group discusses how to forgive and whether forgiveness is the same thing as letting people take advantage of you.

The questions tend to revolve around "What is forgiveness?" And at the end of the night we talk about how we can apply this teaching to our lives. But we need to take it beyond that to help people share their stories and thereby get inside their questions. When this happens, group conversation (both inside and outside the meeting) becomes a lot easier. That's when the soul comes out of hiding and suddenly we're in a place where we see Jesus.

When leading one meeting on the topic of forgiveness, I started out with this icebreaker: "What is your most prized physical possession?" Later in the meeting, after we had talked a little about the freedom of forgiving others, I asked people to imagine that a close friend had harmed their prized possession. Then I asked them to think about and feel their reaction to the situation. Some people offered the "right" Christian response, something like "Of course people are more important than possessions," while others opened up and talked about a time when they were treated in a way that required forgiveness.

Then one member shared a bit more about his relationship with his father, who had been verbally abusive and controlling. This man was struggling with what it meant to forgive his father. We did not have to have answers to his questions. In fact, to provide him with answers—"You need to forgive him in order to be free" or "True obedience and trust of God require that you forgive him"—would have hindered his journey with Christ. He understood what he needed to do. But first he had to work through the questions of "Who am I?" when his identity had been so heavily shaped by his father's abuse. He had to wrestle with his sense of belonging in a world where he did not have to put up with abuse.

No one planned this conversation. The other leaders and I were simply listening for the unexpected surprises of how God might touch people. That's presence.

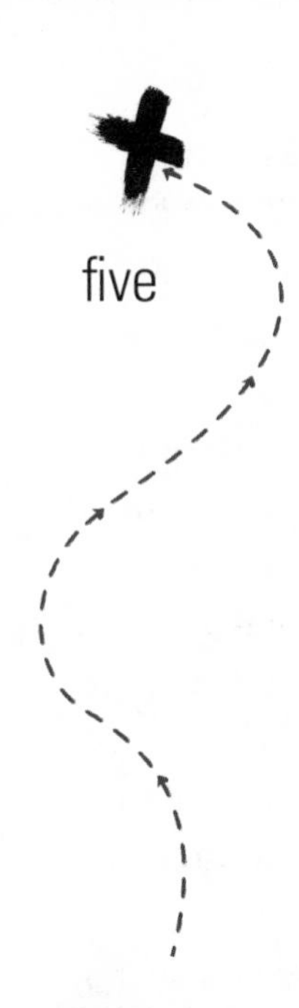

Lead Collaboratively

The Third Practice

Far too many times I've heard this story: "My group is struggling to gain momentum. People like the meetings. But they don't want to contribute anything to the group. I'm having to do all of the work."

Conversations like these point out four common challenges leaders face:

- The leader feels pressure to make the group work.
- The group looks to the leader to make the group work.
- The leader does not do certain tasks very well (such as leading meetings) and so expends inordinate amounts of energy trying to improve that weakness instead of investing energy in what he or she is good at (such as providing care and follow-up during the week).
- Leaders never get a break. They're often tired from leading their group but don't want to tell their pastors because they know how important small groups are to the church.

In the face of these challenges leaders press on, trying not to "become weary in doing good" (Galatians 6:9), striving to overcome their weaknesses and hoping they can become the kind of leader they need to be. While some are able to rise to the occasion, most of the time their groups stay stuck.

The way we lead people is the way people will follow. The group will do as we do, not as we say. If we lead individualistically, then people will follow individualistically. But solo leadership models a way that is contrary to living in community and promotes passivity. Leading people into the way of Jesus is not about doing everything the right way so that small group "consumers" can enjoy the small group "product." The way of Jesus is always collaborative, always participatory. The way of Jesus is cocreated by the entire group in the Spirit, not by the leader on his or her own.

Individualistic leadership begets groups of individualists who will look to the leader to do the right things to make the group work. Individualistic leadership is about production, results and efficiency. In contrast to the solo leader model, groups that advance along the way of Jesus think in terms of collaborative leadership, which occurs on three levels:

- a team within the group
- a team of people who oversee (or coach) the group
- teaming up with other groups

Collaborating in this three-dimensional teamwork structure allows us to break the individualistic mindset that rules our culture by adopting an alternative way that reflects the nature of God.

TRINITY AND TEAMWORK

The trinitarian nature of God has implications for our statements of faith and the teaching in our Sunday morning sermons. In addition, it calls for the church to reflect God's relational and missional nature through small groups and community. But what does the Trinity have to reveal about leadership?

Let me pose it differently: If we did not espouse the Trinity, what would change about how we lead in the church? In my experience, I'm not sure it would make much difference at all. I once heard a church leader speaking on leadership and small groups proclaim, "If you're planning to be a Christian leader, don't get a theological education. Go to business school." While there is value to the wisdom that comes from business schools—many points in this book have been derived from the teachings of noted business writers—this speaker's comment illustrates how he views Christian leadership. He assumes that theology should inform how we live in community and in mission, but he does not think it has anything to do with how we lead.

This point of view is not at all uncommon. For most people, the Trinity belongs to the realm of dogmatic reflection and does not have that much to do with the daily life of the church. There is a great divide between the two (see fig. 5.1).

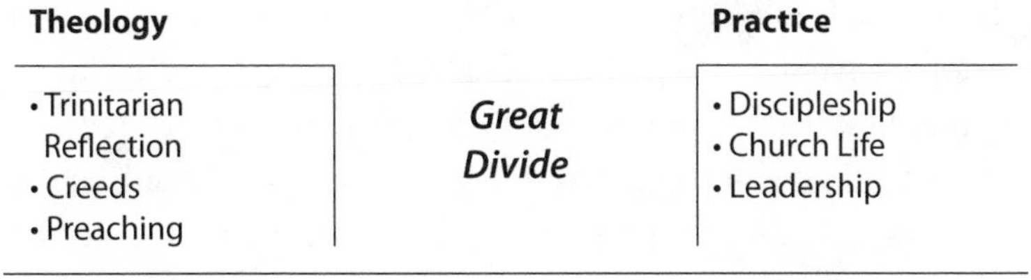

Theology		**Practice**
• Trinitarian Reflection • Creeds • Preaching	***Great Divide***	• Discipleship • Church Life • Leadership

Figure 5.1. A perceived divide

This mindset creates a dualism between theological reflection and the way we lead, which means we have orthodox theology, but there's no such thing as orthodox leadership. We possess ways to measure rightness of our theology but nothing to gauge the rightness of our leadership. As a result we look to pragmatic production to provide a concrete measurement, which means that growth reveals what's right. Growth in groups is the number one way we determine whether leadership is on the right track.

I've seen lots of church leadership driven by an individualistic imagination, and on some levels it's effective—it's easier to get stuff done individualistically. The most obvious example is the superstar preacher model, but it occurs at the small group leader level too. We honor individual leaders who have started the most groups or who have led the longest. We give them prizes. We parade them on stage. And we praise their efforts and how hard they've worked.

If we think a little bit about the triune nature of God, however, we will soon find that many of our common leadership practices don't measure up even if they do produce results. Here's a basic logic for what I'm talking about:

1. We are called to imitate God (Ephesians 5:1).
2. God is triune—Father, Son and Holy Spirit—and lives in eternal unity as three persons in one being. God is a social unity, a community of love, while at the same time each person of the Trinity is unique.
3. God leads out of this character of love. He does not coerce or force anyone for the sake of results. The life of Jesus illustrates this. Jesus led relationally, out of the communion he shared with the Father by the Spirit. And he led by sharing life with others rather than exerting power to get them to think and act according to his plan.
4. Since we are called to imitate God's way of leading, then collaborative leadership is crucial.

COLLABORATION IN THE BIBLE

The language of collaboration is rooted in the Bible. Not only is God a team—Father, Son and Spirit—but this pattern is woven through Scripture. For example, there is no evidence that the New Testament church ever operated with a singular person acting as "chief" leader. Biblical scholar and first-century historian Everett Ferguson writes:

> As in Jewish communities, elders (plural) always appear as a collegial group in Christian congregations (Acts 14:23; 21:18; 1 Tim 4:14; James 5:14; cf. Phil 1:1, "bishops and deacons"). A plural leadership has its own dynamics. A singular leadership is more efficient, so governments and armies want a single commander, and businesses and institutions want a single executive. But Jewish and Christian communities at the turn of the era followed a different pattern. Where the goal is not efficiency but spiritual growth, there a plural leadership offers the advantage of multiple mature examples and the opportunity for understanding and judgment drawn from collective experience.[1]

Likewise, New Testament theologian Gilbert Bilezikian observes, "Whatever leadership structures existed in the early churches, they were inconspicuous, discreet, self-effacing, and flexible. . . . They are invisible servants, whose role is to equip the body."[2]

This leadership of the house churches started by Paul and others was not about hierarchy, determining who was in charge, or leadership recruitment strategies. Leaders led out of their character, their knowledge of God and their love for others. They were people to whom others naturally looked. Michael Green comments on how this kind of leadership would have operated:

> This leadership was always plural: the word "presbyter" from which we derive "priest" is regularly used in the plural when describing Christian ministry in the New Testament. They were a leadership team, supporting and encouraging one another, and doubtless making up for each others' deficiencies.[3]

While the early churches did not operate around the modern idea of a singular leader, some have justified solo leadership because individualistic leaders were predominant in the Old Testament. While true, we must ask if this was God's intent or if he was just working with what was available to him. I would argue that solo leadership was always God's backup plan. From the very beginning God wanted to lead his people through teams. Some might ask, "But what about Moses, David and the other heroes of the Old Testament?" The way Moses led the people was not God's preference. God wanted a "kingdom of priests" (Exodus 19:6) after he led the people out of Egypt, but it became obvious that the Israelites were not ready for that. So God had to work through Moses. Establishing David as the model king was never God's first option. He wanted to be their king (1 Samuel 8). But the people asked for a human king, and God acquiesced.

In some ways, the leadership models of Moses and David are set up as a foil, as a demonstration that even though these were good leaders, individualistic leadership does not result in the way of the kingdom. We can see this in the incarnation. Jesus led in a way that contrasted that of Moses and David. Instead of laws and kingship, he came in servanthood. We see this in John 13 when Jesus washes the feet of his disciples. Triune love is mutual servanthood. The greatest leader becomes the greatest servant. Lesslie Newbigin writes, "The natural man makes gods in his own image, and the supreme God will be the one who stands at the summit of the chain of command. How can the natural man recognize the supreme God in the stooping figure of a slave, clad only in a loincloth?"[4] God led by serving.

Too often we are drawn to the leadership approaches of Moses and David because it's easier to do what they did. Their way of leading more closely lines up with the heroes we elevate in our culture. And then we project that on to God, assuming that's the way he works. Laws and the authority of position get stuff done. And we like it when leaders get stuff done.

The triune way of leading modeled by Jesus does not always get stuff done like we anticipate. And this bothered the disciples. If they were following the Messiah, then he was supposed to produce the results they expected of the Messiah. He was supposed to set up the kingdom by driving out the Romans (as modeled by their great leader David) and restore the temple and God's presence (as modeled by their prototypical leader Moses). But Jesus did not produce what everyone expected.

Leading in a way that reflects the triunity of God is not about producing numbers, although numbers may result. It is about subverting the principalities and the powers of the air—the powers, rulers and authorities that control the normal ways of life in our world. Greg Boyd calls this "power over."[5] The power-over mentality is the way to get stuff done in our culture. Individualistic leaders set up rules and assert their powers to produce results. And when we import this into the church, we allow worldly powers to creep into our life together, with results that look deceptively—and dangerously—godly.

LEADERS LEARN COMMUNALLY

Not only does collaborative leadership reflect the way God leads and works, it also reflects the reality of how we learn. And when I say "learn," I don't mean just learning new information, although that's part of it. I am referring to how we learn new ways of operating. I'm referring to the development of our character—that part of us that comes out whether we intend it to or not. That part of us that's "just the way we are."

Character is developed in community as we are socialized into our practices. Our habits are formed as we pick them up from others. Stanley Hauerwas writes, "The kind of community in which we encounter one another does not merely make some difference for our capacity for agency, it makes all the difference. From this perspective we are not the creators of our character; rather, our character is a gift from others which we learn to claim as our own by recognizing it as a gift."[6]

Who we are is not developed in isolation. We become who we are as we rub shoulders with others. We learn the individualistic way of leading by being around lots of individualistic leaders. We have hundreds of years of experience in which priests, pastors and teaching elders have been called on to be the spiritual individuals who do all things for all people.

As a kid, I learned more about individualism from the church than any other place, especially when it came to leadership. I remember many conversations with people about our pastor and what he needed to do differently for our church to be what it needed to be. He was a very good man and a decent preacher. But he was human like the rest of us. We just did not want him to be human. We lacked a way of operating in which he participated with a team. Nor did his training prepare him for developing a team. This individualistic mentality gets passed down to small groups all over the world. When people don't like the group, the blame gets laid at the feet of the individualistic leader.

If we are going to receive as a gift the character of collaborative leadership initiated by Jesus, we have to learn to do it with one another. To try to do it in isolation makes no sense. It's like trying to become a great cook without ever cooking. We learn alongside one another on the way as we make mistakes. We learn through trial and error when we have a variety of relationships that can speak into the way we lead.

Now let's look at the three dimensions of collaboration.

DIMENSION ONE: A TEAM OF LEADERS WITHIN A GROUP

A few years ago I was overseeing a group that had grown to the point of birthing a new group. As I was praying about the future of that group and how we could help it through its transition, I sensed that the Lord was leading us to wait. During that time of waiting we realized that our approach to group leadership was putting a lot of pressure on one person to be all things to the group. Of course we had leaders in training (interns, apprentices) just like all the small group books advise. But when push came to shove, all the pressure fell on one person. And usually, week after week, no matter how hard we involved others, the rest of the group looked to that one person to do eighty percent of the work.

As a result, we experimented with coleaders. I had not seen much at that point about leading groups this way. The common logic was and is that if you use coleaders, you will have half as many groups. But based on that experiment and follow-up work through the years, I am all the more convinced of the need for team leadership (two to four people) if a group wants to move further along the way of Jesus and be more than a "good meeting" group. Here's what I've observed about creating a leadership team within the group.

First, team leadership relieves the stress on one person to be good at all the things small group leaders do. For instance, when I look at the characteristics and habits of great group leaders, it doesn't take a brain surgeon to see that I'm not very good at many of them. I'm not good at creating a hospitable environment. I'm not great at inviting new people. Nor am I very good at contacting people and being pastoral. My gifts fall into the teacher-prophet category. There are certain things I do naturally and enjoy, while other things I see as a chore.

When I first realized that other people liked doing what I viewed as a chore, I was shocked. I had been operating out of the paradigm that good leaders focus on developing their weaknesses in order to bring them up to an acceptable level. I was expending so much energy on my weaknesses that I did not have energy left to invest in my strengths.

But when you work with a team, you can partner with people who have strengths and gifts that complement your own. You don't have to be good at everything. You get to explore how to lead through your strengths and work with others who have different strengths. For instance, if you are very hospitable and pastoral, you might focus on the responsibilities of leadership that best suit those gifts while someone else facilitates meeting discussion and guides the group in prayer.[7]

Second, team leadership frees leaders from a task focus. Caring for and leading a group of people includes a lot of practical and organizational details. When leadership is shared, the focus can be on the people because the tasks are distributed. Plus, you have an automatic way to keep yourself humble. As a part of a team, you are never *the* leader who makes it work. All successes are shared, as are all failures. But even more, when you work as a team you are required to talk things through and share your perspective with others before simply acting. Team leadership requires mutual submission to one another, and this always generates humility.

Third, team ministry protects leaders from burnout. When I was leading a group solo, I would feel guilty for taking a vacation. I rarely thought about what I needed to be healthy and well-balanced because I felt responsibility for the welfare of the group. With a team, you get to be yourself. You don't have to carry the pressure of constantly being "on" or being strong for the rest of the group. It's much easier to lead in weakness when others are with you carrying the load.[8]

Finally, team leadership empowers the group to be creative about how it will engage people outside the group in mission. Solo-leader groups often struggle to survive. The leader spends a lot of energy just getting the group to show up and connect. But with a team, there is more ownership of the vision and therefore more space for the group to get involved with what God is doing outside the group.

The question facing most small group leaders is "How?" How do we move from this solo group leader mindset to that of a team? In most cases, you cannot just switch from the old way to the next overnight. Here are a few suggestions that can help:

- If you are starting a new group, don't start it until you have a team in place. Don't start the new group and hope to build the team later.
- If you already have a group, begin to test people to see who is ready for more. For instance, you could lead a talk about the various roles members could fulfill and see who steps up. These roles might include some of those listed below. You don't have to fill them all. Put them out there and see who has an interest in what. Then work with these people. Watch to see who follows through and who doesn't.
- When you see a person or two stepping up, begin regular conversations with them about the group. Ask them to start praying about specific aspects of the group's life. Most importantly, ask them what they see as next steps for the group.
- As you progress, ask those who are stepping up to be a part of the leadership team.

Here are some possible meeting roles:

- Study champion: Helps plan future studies and/or serves as one of the facilitators.
- Worship champion: Leads group in worship during meetings, with or without an instrument.
- Host/hostess: Coordinates the meeting places; arrives fifteen minutes early to meetings to welcome others.
- Timekeeper: Gently ensures the meetings begin and end according to the time upon which the group agreed.

- Food champion: Keeps a schedule of who will provide refreshments and snacks.
- Kid's slot champion: Coordinates who will work with the children each week.

Here are some possible group life roles:

- Prayer champion: Encourages prayer and keeps a prayer journal.
- Communications champion: Calls or emails group members to communicate important information.
- Social champion: Plans, involves others and delegates for parties and other times when the group gathers socially.
- Engagement champion: Leads prayer for neighbors, friends, coworkers and family members who need to experience God's love. Challenges group to demonstrate God's love in tangible ways. Not a matchmaker for group members.
- Service champion: Plans group serving opportunities.

DIMENSION TWO: ELDERING

This dimension of collaboration is vertical in nature. Traditionally, a coach or pastor has provided "oversight" to a group leader by providing supervision and counsel. However, a more biblical point of view would refer to this process as "eldering"—the coach or pastor comes alongside the leader as an experienced elder and walks with him or her. There are two aspects to eldering.

Your group needs an elder. Leadership oversight and coaching have been crucial components of small group ministry from its embryonic days. Research has revealed that coaching is crucial. Jim Egli performed an extensive statistical study on what impacts group health and life the most, and the evidence is beyond conclusive: "The single thing that impacts group life more than any other is the ministry of the coach."[9] However, I often find that small group leaders don't want coaching. They find the extra meetings a waste of time. This leaves us with a problem. If leaders need coaching but say they don't want it, we need to ask further questions. Just what is it they don't want? And if coaching has such a huge impact, what part of coaching makes the difference?

Leaders don't want or need a big brother telling them what to do. And they don't want extra meetings to explain lots of theory about what should be happening in their small group. However, they do need the pastor or coach to provide "eldering" for the entire group. Traditionally, the small group world has emphasized the relationship between the coach or pastor and the group leader, urging coaches to focus on supporting and encouraging the leaders. But eldering has a bigger imagination that invests in the people who belong to the group.

The term for elder (*presbyteros*) denotes someone who is older and more experienced. In Jewish culture, it was a common practice for elders to serve their communities, and this practice was carried over into the church. Paul would establish a church, then appoint elders to lead it when he left. To be clear, I'm not using the word "elder" to refer to an official office in church government. I'm talking about it in functional and relational terms.

The New Testament does not provide us with detailed descriptions about how the elders of the early church operated. And I'm not using the word here to try to get back to an early church perspective. Instead, I use it to demonstrate a desperate need within the church for experienced people to guide and lead others. Age is one contributing factor, but experience in walking with the Lord is even more important. Elders have been shaped to be people who can guide others.

Understood this way, eldership should include care and investment into the life of small groups. I've heard it said many times that a coach should not step in and involve himself or herself intrusively in the life of a group. Instead, they should work through the leaders. The same is said about pastors. They should not visit a group because they will step on the authority of the group leader. On one level, this is good advice. Those in official church positions can exert their authority in ways that shut down other leaders. At the same time, when someone is living in a mature, whole walk with Christ and they are serving the church in leadership, why would we restrain them from ministering to the entire group? That just does not make sense.

You need an elder. I'm writing this from Stillwater, Minnesota, the birthplace of our state. One of the buildings here, which now houses little shops and boutiques, used to be a workshop where workers built cars from the ground up. Henry Ford, known for his innovative assembly line, changed all of this. Instead of automobile craftsmen, we now have line workers who assemble automotive replicas one part at a time. From a business perspective, this approach was genius. The various roles along the assembly line were not based on the expertise of any one individual; they were created so almost anyone could do them. The roles became primary. The people filling those roles became secondary because the focus shifted to efficient production.

While serving as a pastor in Canada, I experienced how this Henry Ford mentality can subtly shape the way we oversee group leaders. A family visited our church, and it soon became clear that they had been effective leaders in a church in England. While I listened to the husband share his experience, I began to dream about the small group he and his family could lead. I enthusiastically shared my vision with the man. To my chagrin, he kindly told me they were burned out and needed a place of worship that did not require them to lead. I was disappointed when they went to another church in town.

I was seeing my job as filling roles with leaders and secondarily caring for them. This mindset revealed my assumption that if I somehow filled the roles, the leaders would flourish because they were doing the ministry of the church. I was trying to coach them, but I was doing so with a mentality that put the roles first and the people second. I objectified the people for the sake of the organization. Theologian John Zizioulas challenges this mentality:

> Persons can neither be reproduced nor perpetuated like species; they cannot be composed or decomposed, combined or used for any objective whatsoever—even the most sacred one. Whosoever treats a person in such ways automatically turns him into a thing, he dissolves and brings into non-existence his personal particularity.[10]

As a group leader, you are not an assembly line worker who fulfills a role so that the church can be more effective. You are a person who is valuable to God and loved by God for who you are. And you need an elder who can speak this into your life. This means that you have to allow yourself to be loved like this instead of using your leadership role as a platform to prove yourself to anyone who oversees or directs you. The story of Martha and Mary shines light on this:

> As Jesus and his disciples were on their way, he came to a village where a woman named Martha opened her home to him. She had a sister called Mary, who sat at the Lord's feet listening to what he said. But Martha was distracted by all the preparations that had to be made. She came to him and asked, "Lord, don't you care that my sister has left me to do the work by myself? Tell her to help me!"
>
> "Martha, Martha," the Lord answered, "you are worried and upset about many things, but few things are needed—or indeed only one. Mary has chosen what is better, and it will not be taken away from her." (Luke 10:38-42)

Jesus met with Mary. And Mary met with Jesus. Neither was focused on production or results. They just sat with each other. It's in this space that leaders are developed. It's in this space that leaders are formed.

This has implications for both the group leader and the pastor. First, you are a person first and a leader second. Leadership flows out of who you are. You must be willing to release the need to perform or look good in front of the pastor, elder or coach who serves as an overseer. Second, the one serving as your coach must meet with you as a person first. What does your soul need at this point of your journey? What are your joys? Your struggles? What is the next step for you? These are not questions about how you can be a better leader. These are questions about your soul, and as you receive eldering in these areas, your leadership will naturally advance.

DIMENSION THREE: PARTNERING WITH OTHER GROUPS AND MINISTRIES

The third dimension of collaboration is horizontal. The experiences of small groups around the world during the past fifty years have proven that groups of eight to ten can have an impact on their world. Groups reach unbelievers, they have taken on social initiatives, and they have given up their lives for the sake of others. At the same time, it is wise for a group to join with two or three other like-minded groups to engage their community. Many times the places where God is at work in the local culture require greater investment than what any one group can give. But when two to four groups work together, greater impact is possible.

For instance, a few groups consisting of people who live near one another might organize an annual summer block party and then work together to serve local community needs (we'll discuss this kind of approach further in chapter eight). One church in New Jersey connects three groups at a time to work together on a Habitat for Humanity project. Other groups might adopt a local school and focus on tutoring kids or leading after-school activities.

One way to facilitate this kind of collaboration is to create congregations of three to ten groups. In some cases these congregations meet often—even weekly, as illustrated in *The Connecting Church* by Randy Frazee—but usually they gather less often or on a need-specific basis. For instance, one church I know of organizes these congregations into periodic prayer-walking events. People get to connect with others beyond their small groups and they get to observe what's going on in the community. The same can be done with service projects. Maybe on a Saturday morning several groups work together to offer free oil changes to people in the community who need such a service.

This horizontal collaboration also occurs when one or more groups develop a relationship with organizations or ministries outside the local church. These can include local homeless shelters, ministries for orphans and residences for battered women. I know of some groups who work with specific foreign missions organizations and make annual trips to serve overseas. Some churches provide lists of different ministries so groups can easily discover their options and see where they want to get involved.

PRACTICAL TIP: BIRTH NEW GROUPS OUT OF VISION

Group multiplication has long been a source of stress when it comes to group life. For years it's been taught that groups should multiply when the reach a certain size (usually twelve to fifteen people). But members often find this frustrating—they've spent months or years investing in the other people in the group and now those bonds are being severed. Then they're expected to repeat the bonding and severing pattern in the new group.

A much less taxing way to birth a group is to focus on vision. Don't multiply a group because of size. Multiply because three or four people—a team—feel called by God to launch a new group. As you move forward in your small group, communicate how new groups will be started. If we continually ask God how he is working in us and what he has next for us, then as the group grows, we will discover whom he is raising up to start something new.

LEARNING HUMILITY

Collaboration is a way of embracing the path of humility. It's about realizing that one person or one group cannot do everything. If you lack humility, forcing yourself to collaborate will make a way for it. There's no better way to humble yourself than to put yourself in a team where you have to submit to others. This creates a natural environment where you are free to be who God has made you to be and advance along the way of Jesus.

six

Be Yourself

The Fourth Practice

We love a hero—the kind who possesses abilities no one else has. And this is true in churches all over the place. Our words give us away. I go to "[name of senior pastor]'s church." "I'm part of [name of leader]'s small group." Or "I attend [name of teacher]'s Sunday school class."

Heroic ideals have a deep tradition rooted in the ethics of Aristotle. To him, a hero is the center of the story, one who stands out above others and is self-sufficient, courageous, disciplined, quick-witted, battle-ready and excellent at whatever he does. He does what normal people cannot. He stands against the status quo and leaps into the fray when no else will. He is "great." But there is one more thing that marks a hero. His actions and choices turn out "right." He wins. He succeeds. He is a hero.[1]

Heroic language is full of idealistic words like "radical," "leap of faith," "rejection of the status quo," "irreligious," "subverting the norm," "zealot," "renegade" and so on. And hero language can inspire creative people to experiment with new ways of being the church. Innovative risk takers set the course for others to follow.

However, there's another side to this search for the leadership hero. It can cause us to try to be someone other than ourselves. Instead of being real about the present state of our journey, we try to be at a different place, a more committed place, a more radical place. We try to be heroic.

In contrast to the heroic group leaders we set on a pedestal, we need more leaders who are willing to be themselves, common saints ready to participate in the kingdom way of Jesus.

WILL THE REAL YOU SHOW UP?

Heroes of the way of Jesus don't exist—only saints who live out their real journey with Jesus. This can be hard to understand because heroes are highly visible and saints are not. Our cultural imagination is so shaped by the hero myth that we hear about successful churches and ministries and assume that a hero is at the center of it all.

Let me illustrate by pointing out how Mother Teresa is often portrayed. For years I've heard this remarkable woman's words quoted, her work among the poor in India praised and her impact set up as an example to follow. The picture painted is that of a spiritual giant among spiritual giants. But when you read just a little bit of her story, you realize that there's much more. Her Missionaries of Charity organization includes 610 missions in 123 countries and more than four thousand sisters who worked with her. While there is no doubt that Mother Teresa did some incredible things, the faces and names of these others who served with her are unknown. If you look at the history of the church and the churches that are currently making huge impacts on their communities, it's the unseen, unnamed and unspectacular who are making a difference.

We need leaders who will live as common saints. This is the perspective that Thomas Aquinas promoted as an ethical alternative to that of Aristotle. A saint is one who does not live at the center of the story. A saint's actions are often invisible. A saint lives out of faith and seeks to produce fruit even in weakness and failure instead of trying to live up to some external idea of success. And often a saint's life is characterized by sacrifice. Samuel Wells states, "A hero fears failure, flees mistakes, and knows no repentance: the saint knows that light only comes through cracks, that beauty is as much (if not more) about restoration as about creation."[2]

When saints show up, the soul comes out because saints have no need to pretend. They have no need to hide the cracks because light comes through cracks. The apostle Paul put it this way: "But [God] said to me, 'My grace is sufficient for you, for my power is made perfect in weakness.' Therefore I will boast all the more gladly about my weaknesses, so that Christ's power may rest on me. That is why, for Christ's sake, I delight in weaknesses, in insults, in hardships, in persecutions, in difficulties. For when I am weak, then I am strong" (2 Corinthians 12:9-10).

ALLOWING THE REAL YOU TO BE LOVED

In the opening words of Ephesians, Paul addresses the entire church as "saints" (ESV). We know that these people were far from perfect. They were not living according to their identity, but that did not change the fact that they were saints. Leading people in the way of Jesus involves the leader living out of who he or she already is. We are saints in Christ Jesus. And our call is to offer ourselves to one another—the good, bad and the ugly, knowing full well that we are God's set-apart ones.

I've heard this truth about identity preached hundreds of times. I've preached it myself. However, it often feels like a mental exercise where I have to convince myself of the truth of some kind of dream reality that doesn't have much to do with the way I live. This is because what we're talking about is the root of our being, the ultimate cause of our reality. These questions are addressed in the philosophical discipline of ontology. René Descartes asked these questions and came up with *Cogito ergo sum,* which is Latin for "I think, therefore I am." He determined that his ability to reason was the source of his being.

As I've reflected on how we do life today, I've come to believe there are many other options that lie at the source of our being. While most of us don't ponder these questions in an ontological way, we all live according to a certain ontology. For instance:

- I feel, therefore I am.
- I have fun, therefore I am.
- I work, therefore I am.
- I have power, therefore I am.
- I make money, therefore I am.
- I possess, therefore I am.

I'm sure we could add to this list. For those of us who follow Jesus, we might add something like, "I love, therefore I am." Or we might say, "I follow Jesus, therefore I am." And for leaders in the church, we might posit, "I lead, therefore I am."

As Christians we tend to get our identity out of the fact that we love God and others. We try to do life as Jesus did life. However, there is a problem with this approach. It assumes that the "I" is the source or the cause of "my" being. All of these examples presume that identity is about who "I" am as an individual agent.

Allow me to quote from the great theologian John Zizioulas on this. It's a bit dense but worth the effort:

> Beings exist as particular, therefore, only as gifts of the Other, who grants them an identity by establishing a unique relation with them. In this kind of ontology, in which the Other and not the Self is the cause of being, we not only leave behind the Cartesian ontology of "I think, therefore I am," but we also go

> beyond "I love, therefore I am," since the latter still presupposes the Self as somehow causing being (by love). The proper way of expressing the ontological character of love in an ontology of otherness would rather be: "*I am loved,* therefore I am." Being is a gift of the Other, and it is this very gift that constitutes love; if love does not grant or "cause" a unique identity, it is not true love; it is self-love, a sort of narcissism in disguise.[3]

I am loved, therefore I am. And to be loved is to be loved in relationship. My identity is a gift that arises out of the relationship with the Other (God), which means I'm uniquely loved because my relationship with the Other is different and distinct from the relationship the Other has with anyone else. This is particular love. God loves you in his relationship with you and thereby you are uniquely you in that relationship. You don't need to find your identity in the way someone else has done it. You don't need to live up to some kind of ideal way of being. The real you arises through God's love for you.

ALLOWING THE REAL YOU TO FAIL

The story of Jacob serves as a guide for how we grow into this identity of "I am loved." Jacob was smart. He was good with money. He set goals, and he worked to accomplish those goals. He was not afraid of hard work. He wanted his brother's birthright, so he traded for it. He longed for his father's blessing, so he deceived his father for it. Then he saw a woman. He worked for fourteen years to earn her hand. After this he found a way to get rich, so he made a plan and implemented it.

Then, as the story is written, Jacob headed back home with his wives and children. But his home was not a place of open arms. The last time he'd seen his brother Esau, he'd had to run for his life because he had stolen Esau's birthright. Now, as he entered his homeland, his brother was coming to meet him. To appease Esau, Jacob sent him a gift of 220 goats, 220 sheep, thirty camels, fifty cows and thirty donkeys. When they were young, Jacob had lied. Now that they were older, he would try to buy Esau's love.

Even with this bribe Jacob feared for his life. He was not smart enough, strong enough, rich enough or determined enough to protect himself this time. His walls were crumbling. In Genesis 32:11, Jacob prays to God, "Save me, I pray, from the hand of my brother Esau, for I am afraid he will come and attack me, and also the mothers with their children." But God did much more than that.

On the night before the meeting with Esau, Jacob was alone, and the Bible says "a man wrestled with him till daybreak" (Genesis 32:24). As they wrestled, God touched Jacob's hip and wrenched it. But before Jacob would let him go, he demanded a blessing. So God changed Jacob's name. Instead of being called Jacob, "the deceiver," he would be forever called Israel, or "God-struggler" (literally, "one who wrestles with God"). In fear, Jacob asked God to protect him and bless him. But the blessing did not come as expected.

God did not bless Jacob with strength to meet his brother. He did not give him more money to handle the problem. Nor did he make him smarter. Rather, he made him weaker. God blessed Jacob with brokenness. He brought him to the end of himself and gave him a permanent limp to remind him of his new name and his master.

After this blessing of brokenness, the walls came down between Jacob and his brother. Jacob came in humility and Esau came in forgiveness. God's blessing coincides with brokenness. Often we think we should lead out of strength. "As a leader, I should be smarter than everyone else," we tell ourselves. "I should be stronger and more successful." But God does not want to make us stronger. He wants to make us to live into our weakness and embrace who we are in it. This is the place of blessing! Larry Crabb writes, "Brokenness is a condition, one that is always there, inside, beneath the surface, carefully hidden for as long as we can keep a facade in place. We live in brokenness. We just don't always see it, either in ourselves or in others."[4]

Give me broken leaders over those who lead out of bravado and strength any day. Broken leaders know their limitations. They do not live a lie by trying to be perfect. Only a broken heart can love. Only a person who has come to the end of self can be real. Only a leader with a new name—a spiritual name—will have people following him or her. Just as Jacob was given a new name, so will every leader who walks in the way of Jesus. Names in the Old Testament reflect the character of the person. The Lord will give you new names as you enter brokenness.

When we lead others we face situations that cause us to wrestle with God. These situations are not issues to overcome so that we can get to the real ministry of group life. These situations are the things that drive us into brokenness so we can come to grips with who we truly are as the beloved of God. The rest of this chapter identifies some of these common situations.

WHEN (NOT IF) GROUP MEMBERS CAUSE PROBLEMS

Here's a sure thing for any small group: you will have problems. There will be at least one person in every season of group life that creates—well, let's call them "challenges." Groups are full of people. And all people are hurting and need healing in some way. When people start revealing themselves to one another, their hurts will hurt others. Hurting people hurt people, as the old saying goes.

These hurts manifest in as many different ways as there are people in groups. However, I've observed some consistent patterns over the years. They are illustrated by figure 6.1.

Figure 6.1. Individual dysfunction patterns

A fun activity is to name each of the people represented in this picture. For instance, the owl at the top could be called Mr. I-Know-the-Answer-but-I'm-Not-Telling. Or Mr. I've-Done-This-Before-So-I-Can't-Be-Bothered. Of course this illustration is all men. Women don't display dysfunctions like these in groups. Right? Well, since I'm a man I won't respond.

Most of the time people's hurts don't come out all at once. But when one does, a leader's response can be the difference between letting the problem control the group and allowing the Spirit to use the situation to lead the group to the next level. So when problems occur, here are a few questions to ask:

- Is this a new behavior or just an outward manifestation of an ongoing problem? If it is new, then find out what has happened in the person's life and talk through the issue. If it is ongoing, then it may be time to deal with the issue and see God's healing.
- Is this best addressed with the entire group, in a sub-group of two or three or in a one-on-one conversation? Don't assume that there is a one-size-fits-all solution.
- Does this person need help from someone outside the group? Sometimes issues arise that are bigger than what you or the group can deal with. Enlist the help of your coach or pastor.
- What is God doing through this problem to change the person? What is God doing to change the group? Remember this is not about fixing the issue. God wants to work through that which arises to change our lives.
- What is God doing in you as you relate to the person who is struggling? This may be the most important question of all. If you go forth in ministry in humble submission, the person who is presenting the challenge—and the rest of the group as well—will be much more likely to respond in kind. This starts on your knees, asking God to give you his heart for the situation.

A few years ago I was leading a group with a Mr. Know-It-All. He reminded me of the person at the bottom of the picture with the raised hand and pointed finger. He had answers for everyone's problems. And he was driving me crazy. Then I realized that the person who needed to change the most was me. I needed God's heart for him. As I prayed, I did not feel that he was ready for direct confrontation or challenge. However, I was given the grace to steer his comments in the group meetings without an angry face. And after a while, he loosened up and quit being so Know-It-All-ish. All he needed was some time. But I had to change first.

WHEN (NOT IF) YOU ARE NOT GOOD AT LEADING THE GROUP

As you lead, you will find that there are things you're good at doing and other things you stink at. Over the years I've found it helpful to learn more about how God has made me and my unique personality, including my strengths and weaknesses. I've worked through multiple personality profiles, including the DiSC, Myers-Briggs and StrengthsFinder programs. And I have processed the results with others who know me. I've often found that when something comes as a surprise to me, others wonder why it's taken me so long to figure it out.

Many leadership books and programs fail to recognize that people are different. They simply propose a plan that should work for all. But the reality is that their findings and suggestions work because more people are wired with personalities and strengths that fit those patterns. For instance, in the DiSC profile, sixty-nine percent of the population is a high S, which is characterized by steady commitment, consistency and routine. Therefore one could find that certain leadership practices are more effective simply because more leaders in the world happen to have the personality traits that naturally fit those practices. But when a person who is a high D, which stands for dominant, daring and directive, tries to implement the standardized practices that work for a high S, it will feel like a man trying to wear a bra.

So find out who you are, how you are wired, what you like to do and what you don't. God works through how he made you. Too many times we assume that we need to develop what we're not good at to a more acceptable level. That used to be my approach. Then I realized that I was horrible at administration and anything that had to do with food. I also wasn't very good on the phone and hated inviting people to activities. So when I tried to do these things in my group, they always flopped. But those were the things

I was told I needed to be good at. Now, I'm free to be a dreamer, think about vision and the future, teach people about God's ways and create environments where people are free to have conversations with one another. I don't have to be good at everything a group needs in a leader. I can depend on my strengths.

WHEN (NOT IF) DISCOURAGEMENT HITS

With leadership comes discouragement. In fact, let me so bold as to say that if you never experience times of discouragement, you most likely are not taking any risks. Or you don't care that much. But if you don't care, you most likely aren't reading this book.

Discouragement is part of leading. You will hit walls when you don't know what to do. Your group will go through times that make you want to give up. People will disappoint you. And you will disappoint yourself.

What do you do with this? Let me suggest a few things I've learned about discouragement through the years of leading.

First beware of the temptation to ignore the reality of what you are facing. Avoid the tendency to ignore your discouragement. Some will tell you to have faith, to get back in touch with the vision, to claim God's promises and to act as if there is not a problem. When we do this we are not dealing with reality. God knows where we are on the journey and wants to meet us in our discouragement.

Second, learn to be honest about what you are discouraged about. Really honest. Take it to God. Share it with a friend, a pastor or a coach. God's leaders are "wounded healers" and you don't have to pretend to be more than you are.

In the midst of this honesty, the third step is to ask God what he wants to do in you. The situation that is causing your discouragement is not a problem to be fixed. It's an opportunity for you to meet God in a new way. What is God saying to you in the midst of the discouragement?

The fourth action may the hardest: wait. Be still. Make room in your life for the Spirit to transform you. Every time discouragement has hit me, my natural tendency is to want to get over it quickly and get back to doing what I know to do. But when I finally wise up and slow down, I sense God working deep within my soul in a new way.

Fifth, act in faith. Grab the vision. Walk in hope of a new future. Claim God's promises. Fight. But know this—you will fight in a different way.

WHEN (NOT IF) YOU DON'T KNOW WHAT TO DO

Someone raises a question you don't know how to answer. Someone confesses a sin that's a bit bigger than you expected. People quit coming to meetings. Or meetings just fall flat. You find yourself not knowing what to do next. Where do you turn? How do you respond?

First of all, recognize that you are not alone. Every time I come up against something I don't know how to handle, loneliness sets in. I feel like I'm the only one in the world facing this issue. And that feeling never helps. But when you realize you're not alone, there is freedom to admit you don't know what to do. And that's a good place to be.

The second thing to do is pray. The best way to learn how to lead is to face unknown situations head on. Sometimes we think that the best way to lead better is to learn a new technique or seek advice from someone else. However, I've found that I have to go to God first and let him teach me. I have to face my inadequacies directly and see what needs to change in me. This requires that we pray *through* the situation, as opposed to just praying *for* the situation. We pray all the way through what we need to learn until we learn it.

A third option is to ask for help. I remember the first time I had a group member confess a major sexual sin to me and a coleader. We prayed for him. We affirmed him. We did all we could for him. But his need was bigger than we could handle. We needed the help of other leaders. And because we did not seek this help quickly, we got bogged down in his problems. The fact that we did not know what to do weighed heavily on us. We needed the counsel of someone who had been down this path before.

Most of what we learn as leaders happens on the job and just in time. It would be nice if we could just download a huge set of information up front and then go and be a great leader. But that's not how it works. It reminds me of how I learned farming as a kid. I learned by farming with my dad, my uncle and my grandfather. Often when I was given a task, I'd come up against something I did not know how to do. Sometimes I'd work at it and figure it out. Most of the time I'd ask for advice or help.

When we're leading a group, we will always face new challenges that we won't know how to handle. There is no encyclopedia for group leaders that covers all situations. We're talking about leading people, and every group is unique. As we face challenges, we have opportunities to trust God in new ways. And we can grow in our ability to love others.

WHEN (NOT IF) YOU ENCOUNTER PERSONAL STRUGGLES

I wish there were a set of clear-cut rules and steps that would keep us on a path free from personal struggles, where we could jump from one victory to the next. I remember when I first started leading a group. The expectation was for each group to multiply regularly, at least once per year. When I did the math, I imagined the potential impact my leadership would have on people. I envisioned all kinds of victories in my ministry.

Then something happened. It's called life. Struggles occurred that impeded the great success I had hoped for. I found myself taking three steps forward and two steps back. I found myself walking through the valley of the shadow of death. Following Jesus in this life involves ups and downs. On the path of following Jesus and therefore on the path of leading others, there will be mountains and valleys. It's just the way it goes.

Some of the valleys and failures are due to our choices. But they aren't always rooted in sin or moral failure. They also come as a result of living in a world that falls short of God's kingdom. Sometimes life just kicks us in the stomach. Maybe you lose a job and have to file for bankruptcy. Or your son tells you that his girlfriend is pregnant. Or your spouse gets sick. And there go your plans for how you thought your leadership would work. Questions arise. Pain sets in. You might even find yourself in a place of darkness and depression.

Of course struggles also come from poor choices. None of us is perfect and until the day Jesus returns, leaders will need to deal with that fact. Sometimes our choices are huge, catastrophic and immoral, like sexual indiscretion. Other times we make choices that reveal character flaws, like blasting someone with anger.

Whatever the case, life and leadership involve personal struggle. And too often Christian leaders feel expectations that they should not struggle. We love to train our leaders to create safe places in their groups for people to share their struggles. But we must also create safe places where leaders can struggle without fear of judgment or condemnation. Since we never outgrow the struggles of life, we must ask if our leaders have places where they experience this kind of safety.

This goes far beyond creating a place where leaders can talk together or telling leaders they can be transparent. This is about church culture. If a church is shaped by a culture of performance, then sharing about personal struggles will be very difficult for people. There will be a focus on external expectations and rule-following. But if the culture of the church is one where messy life together is an expectation, where everyone is given the space to struggle together, then leaders are going to be much more likely to open up.

We are all wounded. And we will all be wounded further. The greatest leaders of the church have recognized this reality and allowed God to work through their wounds to touch others. God works through wounded healers. He does not work around the wounds. He does not work in spite of the wounds. He redeems the wounds for the sake of the world. It's backward logic from the way we commonly see it, but nonetheless it's God's mysterious way of working. God redeemed the world through the wounds of Jesus, and it still works that way today.

WHEN (NOT IF) BURNOUT COMES KNOCKING

If you are a leader, there will be times when the ministry needs you face will be more than you can handle. The group grows and the new members have lots of questions. So you have them over for meals. You have two people who are potential group leaders. So you start meeting with them for coffee every week. The group is excited about reaching out to some people who live nearby. So you help organize a regular cookout, even hosting one yourself. Then of course there are those three people in the group who always need extra attention.

Then it hits you. You wake up and you don't want to do the work. You don't want to prepare the lesson for the upcoming meeting. You don't want to answer the phone. You don't want to organize or even attend the next activity. You're burned out. Now what do you do?

First of all, slow down. Since you are not the answer to the needs of the world, you can give yourself permission to take a deep breath and rest. Of course, this assumes that you know how you rest best. Many leaders do not know how to rest and what kind of rest best suits them. Do you need a retreat? Does taking a walk in nature help? Some find reading helpful.

Second, talk to your coach or pastor about what you are feeling. Push aside any guilt you might feel about it.

Third, focus your ministry on your strengths and your gifts. You don't have all of the gifts of the Spirit. If you don't know how God primarily works through you, then find out. Talk with others about how they see God moving through you.

Fourth, get some help. You don't have to lead your group alone. Delegate some of the responsibilities to others. One of the worst assumptions I've made as a leader is that I had to do everything, including the stuff I was bad at doing. There are people who want to help and they actually enjoy doing the stuff you don't like to do. Talk to them and find out how they can help.

Fifth, take a weekly Sabbath. Too many people involved in Christian ministry do not know how to let go of their responsibilities one day a week. A weekly Sabbath teaches us to trust God and to pay attention to the ways he is working without us.

In no way is this some kind of recipe for getting out of burnout. In my experience, the only way out is to struggle through it. The patterns that lead to burnout usually need to be replaced by other patterns. These five things can help you develop new patterns that will lead to more effective ministry.

WHEN (NOT IF) YOU ARE TEMPTED TO COMPLAIN

It's easy to be thankful when everyone shows up to our meetings, when people are growing and maturing and when the group is committed to loving those who don't know God's love. But leaders of character know that the time to be most thankful for the people they lead is when these things are not happening. They are thankful simply because the people they lead are loved by God. They are thankful not because the people are doing the right things but because they are prized children in God's family.

Often church leaders are professional complainers. And it seems to me that progressive and innovative leaders take this to a new level, complaining about the state of the church and the mediocrity of our people. If we want to change things, we won't do so with a character shaped by complaining.

When you are tempted to complain, use that as a reminder to be thankful. Thank God for the people in your group. Thank him for what you are learning from the difficulties. And thank him for what he is doing that you don't yet see.

Then go stark-raving mad and lay out all of your complaints to God. Tell him how you feel. Complain away. God can handle it.

EMBRACING WHO YOU ARE

Being yourself is about making space in your life for the Spirit to grow you up as walk with Jesus on the way. This is God's way, God's unfolding story of the redemption of all things. The Father-Son-Holy Spirit is the main actor. I've got a bit role, but when I really see what the Father, Son and Spirit are doing in the world, my role takes on huge significance. My life matters. I become a change agent for kingdom life, but not because I get it right all the time. Sometimes I do and sometimes I don't. This is the mystery of how God works. God works through me and beyond me at the same time. And when I allow myself to be drawn into this mystery, I more fully enter into and embrace the truth of my common sainthood.

Most of this journey along the way is more mystery than I'd like. The ability to embrace who I am may be nine parts mystery and one part effort on my part. If I don't offer my one part, I miss out on most of the nine parts of mystery. (In other words, this is no excuse for laziness.) My one part is not about trying to focus my attention more and more on what I need to be doing and how I need to apply some nugget of truth. My one part is to focus my heart, soul, mind and strength on the mysterious story of God's salvation of the world. And as I allow this story to shape me, my actions change. I relinquish control. My love grows organically. I live into the kind of person I was created to be.

Then as I journey with Jesus and others in my ability to just be myself, I am more and more free to be with people, to love them and serve as a discipling leader who shares his life with God's people.

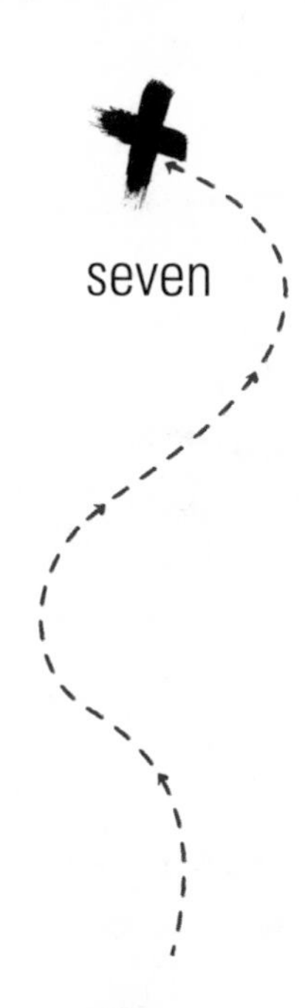

seven

Hang Out

The Fifth Practice

Suppose that in the year 2222, a historian who specializes in early twenty-first-century life is asked to write a history book about our current decade. While most historians focus on headline news issues like war and politics, her interest lies elsewhere. She is seeking to understand how average people, those who didn't typically make the news, lived on a daily basis. She focuses on everyday life to determine how everyday people do everyday stuff. For her research, she has a new innovation, a special computer that allows her to observe, like a running movie, one person for one week of their life. After watching a hundred different weeks as lived out by a hundred individuals, she is able to compile a list of words that describe how people live. What words do you think she would come up with?

When I lead this exercise at seminars, participants shout out words and phrases like

- fast-paced, frenzied, time-crunched
- controlled by fear
- lonely, isolated

- fast-food-oriented
- productive
- exciting, exhilarating
- unsettled, transient
- technology-driven
- focused on television
- rootless, transient
- far from family

Then I ask the group to identify words that this historian might use to describe interpersonal relationships in our day. The list always includes

- geared to avoid conflict
- paper-thin
- too numerous
- surface-y
- overwhelming
- short-term
- social media-driven
- nice

These words describe the common cluttered life that dominates our culture. During the many times I've led groups through this exercise, I've never had anyone list words like "joyful," "restful," "fulfilled" or "at peace." Nor has anyone ever mentioned that relationships are full of fun, sharing, depth, connections or commitment. Yet these are the words that describe the stuff that makes life rich.

When we see people living this way—in contrast to the cluttered patterns—we are drawn to them, as if their lives were works of art.

Consider the most popular sitcoms of the last sixty years: *The Honeymooners, I Love Lucy, M.A.S.H., Sanford and Son*s, *Cheers, Friends, Seinfeld, Martin* and *The Big Bang Theory*. These stories revolve around characters relating to one another in fulfilling, uncluttered ways through the ups and downs of life. They are actually living out a type of beauty in the midst of doing a lot of nothing.

I hope and pray that you are reading this thinking that your life does not reflect the clutter listed above. I hope that your life and relationships are full of what the Hebrew Bible calls *shalom*, which we often translate as "peace." But the English word "peace" does not quite do it justice. When we think about being peaceful, we either imagine inner well-being or something that happens to us when we're sitting by a river without any commitments. Aaron's priestly benediction is helpful here:

> The LORD bless you
>   and keep you;
> the LORD make his face shine on you
>   and be gracious to you;
> the LORD turn his face toward you
>   and give you peace [*shalom*]. (Numbers 6:24-26)

A better translation for *shalom* might be "wholeness." Old Testament theologian Walter Brueggemann reflects, "*Shalom* is perhaps the quintessential mark of infinity, a continuing state of communal well-being that is wide and deep and sustainable. The *face* yields *shalom*."[1]

I pray that your life is characterized by the wholeness of beauty, the fullness of life that comes from experiencing the face of God and not the unsustainable clutter that prevails over most people's days and weeks. If that is the case, then share your life with others. Demonstrate how you live to those of us who too quickly get caught up in the rat race of trying to keep up. What you have is a rare gem, a prized possession that makes life worth living. Instead of a cluttered soul, you have a spacious soul, which means you have room to love and be loved.

This space in your soul clears the clutter so you can simply be with others, whether your family, your group, or your friends and neighbors. *Shalom* creates winsome beauty in your soul that can be shared with others as you simply walk with them in the everydayness of life.

The best small groups are those that refuse to embrace the clutter. Instead they find creative ways to make sure their souls have enough space for God and one another by prioritizing the value of "hanging out"—that is, doing nothing together. This is where discipleship happens. When we hang out, we can observe how another person loves God and others in the regular stuff of life. We can then see where we're lacking in love, which pushes us to the feet of God to get it from him. The way of Jesus is full of eating together, conversations about interests, and time together when we're not looking at the clock. In this context we see God working through others and drawing us along the way.

SQUEEZING OUT THE SOUL

A few years ago I was listening to a sermon in which the pastor led his listeners in a reflection exercise. He instructed us to sit quietly and reflect on the fact that God was present with us. Then we were to ask God if he wanted to show us something or say anything to us. Over the next thirty seconds I saw a picture that tore me up. I saw myself as a very old man in a hospital room, and it was obvious I was nearing the end. My wife and four kids entered the room. We were happy to see one another and it was obvious that we shared good relationships. But something was lacking. I focused on my oldest son Deklan. While we did not have a bad relationship, I knew it was not what it could have been. I had not loved him in the ways he needed to be loved.

As this vision played in my imagination like a short film, I wept because I knew it was true. Deklan and I have very different personalities. He loves fun, long stories and is very extroverted. I am serious, intentional and very introverted. And I was hitting a wall about how to connect with him.

At the time I had this experience with God, I was very, very busy, mostly with ministry commitments. A lot was pressing on me and I was being pulled in far too many different directions. I was perpetually tired, both emotionally and physically. I felt unfulfilled, even though I was doing all the right ministry stuff for God. Clutter, clutter, clutter. Within seconds I realized I needed to change some life patterns to make room in my soul to be with my children, to hang out with others, and to lead my group in a way that honored the fullness of life.

As I work with pastors and leaders to help them develop small groups, we consistently have conversations about these themes, usually centered around the fact that people don't have enough time to live in community and engage in God's mission. Their questions go like this:

- How do people have enough time to lead a group?
- How much time can we expect people to volunteer when they're so busy?
- What do we do when our most qualified leaders are already overcommitted?

The pressures of work, the kids' activities, the pull of social media and packed calendars stretch us far and wide. And often those who are the most committed to God find themselves stretched the most. The faithful church leaders who show up for everything are called on to serve in more and more ways precisely because they are so faithful. Those who have the most to offer relationally are often stuck in committee meetings or sitting in two to three worship services per week.

Moving up the church leadership ladder often looks like the opposite of *shalom,* and small group leadership often follows this path. We have trained leaders to add group leadership to their overly busy lives, thus leaving little time for being human with one another. Church council meetings, discipleship programs, training sessions and other requirements are all treated as additional tasks that need to be accomplished. We just add small group stuff to this list.

A TIME PROBLEM

Many have wrestled with these questions, and for the most part the answers come in some form of simplicity. While simplicity is crucial—and I will offer some insight along these lines toward the end of the chapter—often the way we approach simplicity works against us. We cut out some clutter from our lives by removing some activities, only to add other activities that look more kingdom-like. Yet our lives remain cluttered. We replace one kind of busyness for another.

There are some great techniques out there for managing time more effectively, and I've found many of them helpful. However, reorganizing our calendar will not get us very far down the way of Jesus. In other words, I'm not saying you need to pull out your calendar and cut out other activities so you can replace them with "hanging out." That's not the way hanging out works. Hanging out occurs when we make room for each other so we don't have to look at the clock or squeeze people in between other commitments.

This requires us to think about how we view time, not just how we use time. Samuel Wells, an Anglican priest and writer of many books on ethics, has made some of the most astute observations I've ever encountered about how people in our culture relate to time:

> For many people, time is a commodity. It is treated like one of the most valuable things money can buy. People who are busy and important use commodity-language to describe time. They "buy" time, or "spend" time; they talk of "using" time, or even of "investing a great deal of time," or sometimes of "putting time aside"; they "save" time or "waste" time, "lose" time or "find" time. Not any old time; they are only interested in "quality" time. All of these words treat time as a product, like something one could buy in the supermarket. Occasionally it is pointed out that "time is money." It is considered a very good thing in these circles to save time—though it is not always clear how one is to spend the time one has saved.
>
> Another group of people would love to be busy and important, but for a variety of reasons they feel that they are not. Yet because commodity-language is the way so many people speak of time, this second group are made to feel that because they are not in a hurry, they are "wasting" time, or "losing precious time" in life's race. For these people, time quickly becomes an enemy. Because the commodity-language does not fit, they often use battle-language. Time is "against" them, or "presses in on" them; it "weighs heavy" on their lives. They seem to be failing the "test" of time. The saddest language is that which speaks of "killing" time, since those who set out to kill time almost always lose the battle.[2]

The words we use about time reveal what we believe about how God works in the world. There are those who control time to make things happen. And there are those who are controlled by time where things happen to them. For twenty-five years I've interacted with various streams of small group life—ideas about missional small groups, church life, church vision, missional community, evangelism and so on—and in most of these areas we've assumed that the role of the leader is to either keep control of time or become someone who controls time.

Activism and results get attention. Getting something done for God and his mission is the call to valor. Leaders who get it done and get it done quickly are venerated. I remember a mentor from my past saying, "Time is like money. Once it's spent, it's gone." This was stated in the midst of a talk on evangelism. The implication was that we had work to do and we were wasting time if we were not winning souls and growing groups.

This commodification of time is the way of our culture. When someone responds to the question "How was your day?" with "Busy!" or "I'm exhausted from all the work," we see this as a mark of accomplishment. I know that I've responded this way with a sense of pride and superiority, as if to say, "Look at me; I'm needed." And if we say we're busy in ministry stuff, our standing goes up even higher.

But frenetic, overwhelmed leaders will not change the world. They only replicate the pattern of our cluttered culture using different words. The way I live is the way people will follow. If I lead out of clutter because I view time as a commodity to produce results for God's kingdom, then people will follow in a way that follows suit. Jean Vanier writes:

> But to be good instruments of God's love we must avoid being over-tired, burnt-out, stressed, aggressive, fragmented or closed up. We need to be rested, centred, peaceful, aware of the needs of our body, our heart and our spirit. Jesus says that there is no greater love than to give our lives, but let us not give our over-tired, stressed and aggressive lives. Let us, rather, give joyful ones![3]

If leaders are leading out of stress, the need to produce and a feeling of being overwhelmed, they are leading in a way that is not sustainable. It might work for the programmatic aspects of church life. We can pull off all kinds of church programs in a frenetic way. But small groups depend on life-giving patterns that come from spacious souls. Time is not a commodity for production. It is a gift in which the future of God—when God's full reign is completely manifest—enfolds back on the present by the power of the Spirit. It is the future that Christ began when he came, a realm in which God is already at work in ways we cannot fully see or know. It is God's time, not our time, and he is at work in time. We are not producing the kingdom; we are participating in it. This kind of participation requires that our souls line up with how God works in time.

WHAT THE SOUL NEEDS

God made us to work in his time, not against it. This is most clearly seen in the way our souls operate. We all have longings of the soul, the stuff that lies beneath our small talk and under our opinions and ideas. In our souls we have dreams, fears, desires and disappointments. It's the part of us that wants to come out from behind the bushes and ask, "Will you embrace this part of me?" Or, "Can I be the real me with you?"

For most of us, the soul is shy. It cannot be rushed. While we preach about the need for transparency with other believers, we cannot force the soul to come out and play. Either we feel safe or we don't. Transparency happens when people take off their masks and let others see parts they don't usually share. When this occurs, groups enter into a completely different zone of life together. To get to this point, we must understand what our souls need. In his book *A Hidden Wholeness*, Parker Palmer comments about this:

> Unfortunately, community in our culture too often means a group of people who go crashing through the woods together, scaring the soul away. . . . We preach and teach, assert and argue, claim and proclaim, admonish and advise, and generally behave

> in ways that drive everything original and wild into hiding. Under these conditions, the intellect, emotions, will, and ego may emerge, but not the soul: we scare off all the soulful things, like respectful relationships, goodwill, and hope.[4]

As an alternative, Palmer invites groups to learn to sit quietly together in the woods and "wait for the soul to show up." This takes time, patience and a refusal to force people into transparency. Let me say it again: time and patience are essential. The practice of patience is crucial to the way of Jesus. God has never been in a hurry to change the world—just consider how long he worked in the history of the Old Testament between Adam and Jesus. If I were in charge, I would have tried to fix the world much more quickly. Yet Jesus came in the "fullness of time." God did not force his kingdom on his people because "love is patient" (1 Corinthians 13:4). God knows that love is not something that can be forced on others.

While we all long to be loved through the honest sharing of our souls with one another, we all have histories that cause us to hide and shun love. No amount of moralizing about the importance of transparency will change that. No grand teaching on the need to be a disciple and get serious about following God will roll out the red carpet for the soul. Vanier shares about this from his decades of experience in community life:

> Each person with his or her history of being accepted or rejected, with his or her past history of inner pain and difficulties in relationships with parents, is different. But in each one there is a yearning for communion and belonging, but at the same time a fear of it. Love is what we most want, yet it is what we fear the most. Love makes us vulnerable and open, but then we can be hurt through rejection and separation. We may crave for love, but then be frightened of losing our liberty and creativity. We want to belong to a group, but we fear a

> certain death in the group because we may not be seen as unique. We want love, but fear the dependence and commitment it implies; we fear being used, manipulated, smothered and spoiled. We are all so ambivalent toward love communion and belonging.[5]

If our lives are full of clutter, our souls will hide. And if we clutter up our small groups with activities, goals and good intentions, we might make tangible progress but our souls will recede.

When I was in my late twenties, I initiated a small group that met at a coffee shop. Since I was leading this gathering, I introduced some guidelines so that our group would have a common vision and practice. The guys just looked at me with blank stares. I was trying to be intentional about our meetings so that we would grow as disciples. I wanted us to live into community and mission.

Little did I realize that my intentionality was getting in the way of our souls. I was turning the guys in my group into objects who were present for the sake of my intentions. In other words, I was putting my desires for objective results like group growth, discipleship and mission ahead of the people. Thankfully, they were smarter than I was and understood that the soul emerges when we learn to "hang out."

And when the soul emerges, we see the outcomes of growth, discipleship and mission. It is an organic overflow that arises from simply being with each other, having enough room in our souls that we have space for each other.

IDOLS OF OUR CLUTTERED SOUL

In the late 1990s, I met a missionary friend at the Houston airport during his five-hour layover. At the time he was serving in Ecuador and had helped develop thousands of small groups. As we talked we did not accomplish anything. Instead we shared stories, talked about dreams and just hung out. He commented, "In South America, people do this kind of thing every day."

I responded, "We don't in America. What if our job is not so much about leading small groups as it is about learning to be with each other in the stuff of life?"

While every culture has its own barriers to the Jesus way, including South America, this story helps us see a specific struggle we face in the United States. Most other cultures around the world are group-based and it's much easier for them to see the value of hanging out with one another. Being together is part of life, generating self-worth and identity. In contrast, those of us shaped by Western culture think in terms of the individual first, so we do not naturally see the value of hanging out. Instead our sense of self-worth and identity is shaped by what "I" experience as an autonomous individual. This produces idols that clutter our souls. These idols are

- my position
- my power
- my possessions
- my pleasure

The more our sense of well-being is tied to any of these things, the more we will invest in them, and the more effort, energy, time and stress they will require of us. Our time is not just filled with commitments on a calendar. It is filled with having to manage these idols. To call into question the value of these idols is to call into question what makes our culture tick.

To combat these idols, we challenge them. We preach about how they destroy lives. We call people to a higher focus. We even provide people practical tips for moving beyond them. And we get in small groups where we commit to love one another and participate in

God's mission. But the group struggles to open up. Individuals start making excuses to miss. The energy in the meetings wanes.

So leaders try to fix the problem. Common approaches include:

- Call people to a higher level of commitment.
- Get a new curriculum.
- Take a break for the summer.
- Have a party.
- Get some training on how real groups should operate.
- Create short-term groups that let people switch groups on a regular basis.
- Create accountability groups that meet weekly to talk about a list of questions that deal with issues we don't normally discuss in group meetings.

While there is some merit to all of these things—I've seen each one help a group take their experience up a notch—none of them get to the core issues and how these idols shape our identity. So they usually provide only short-term results.

We have to deal with the fact that these idols are at war with community. If these four idols are progressively advancing in my life, then Western culture tells me I am succeeding, and my identity and sense of well-being increase. To invest in these idols requires time, energy and effort, and anyone who cannot help me attain position, power, possessions or pleasure is undermining the idols. As a result, a group that doesn't help me in these areas gets in the way of my sense of well-being as defined by the idols. In his book *The Relational Being*, Kenneth Gergen states:

> If the self is primary, then relationships are secondary in their importance to us. We must be forever cautious about connection. Relationships will inevitably place demands on the

> individual; expectations and obligations will develop; norms of right and wrong will be imposed. If we are not very careful, our freedom will be destroyed. . . . If we see relationships as secondary and artificial, we will seek them out primarily when they are required for our personal use or satisfaction. In this sense, a committed relationship is a subtle mark of insufficiency. It suggests that we lack something. We are so vulnerable that we sacrifice our autonomy.[6]

The idols of position, power, possessions and pleasure add clutter to our lives, and they require more clutter in order to provide a sense of individualistic well-being. The best way to get more from these idols is to buy into the trap of more work, more effort, more activity. Therefore, making space in our souls necessarily competes with these idols that shape our modern sense of identity and self-worth.

Our souls long for and need the space and freedom to peep out, like a flower slowly unfolding in spring, but our cluttered souls are addicted to idols that convince us we need to pull the flower open so we can get to the next thing. In order to create space for our souls to emerge, we cannot go on the warpath against the four idols. They are simply the natural, logical consequences of an identity that is shaped by individualistic autonomy. Rather, we must reframe how identity works. We must rethink how we see ourselves.

DECLUTTERING IDENTITY

Typically, when we consider personal identity within a biblical perspective, we begin with "my" personal relationship with God. So I turn to the Bible to discover what God has said about me. For instance:

- I am . . . a child of God (Romans 8:16).
- I am . . . redeemed from the hand of the enemy (Psalm 107:2).

- I am . . . forgiven (Colossians 1:13-14).
- I am . . . saved by grace through faith (Ephesians 2:8).
- I am . . . justified (Romans 5:1).
- I am . . . sanctified (1 Corinthians 6:11).
- I am . . . a new creation (2 Corinthians 5:17).
- I am . . . a participant in his divine nature (2 Peter 1:4).

When I as an individual embrace these truths about myself, they can reshape how I perceive my relationship with God. However, the basic way these types of identity lists work is rooted in a specific understanding of the gospel, a message of good news of personal salvation for individuals. In this understanding, salvation is primarily shaped by a vertical imagination about me and God. And while developing a healthy sense of salvation identity through an understanding of who I am in Christ can help me overcome self-deprecating lies about who I am, it does not help us combat the idols that clutter our souls. It can actually keep us mired in autonomous questions like:

- How can I get my relationship right with God?
- Where can I find a church or small group that will benefit me?
- What are some ways that I can be a good evangelist or make a difference in the world?

While these questions are not inherently wrong, they are limiting. They illustrate a view of personal identity very different from that shaped by a biblical imagination. For instance, if someone with the perspective of the Hebrew Scriptures were to define personal identity and well-being, he would discuss a three-way relationship among God, the tribe to whom he belonged, and the land in which he lived. This three-way identity relationship might be illustrated with a triangle (see fig. 7.1).

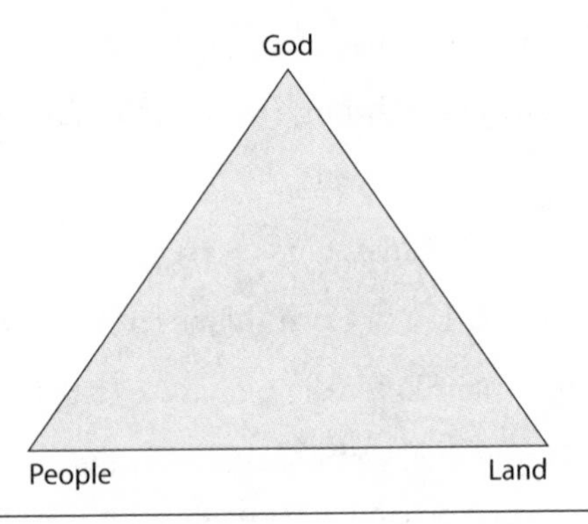

Figure 7.1. Three-way identity relationship

For instance, if you were born during the times of Abraham, Isaac and Jacob, you would have been shaped by a relationship between these three elements. God (or in the case of other peoples, a "god") was crucial to a person's self-perception. Who people worshiped shaped who they were. For us moderns this is not that hard to understand. But the next two are.

Ancients were also shaped by their belonging to a specific people, tribe or family. Their identity could never be separated from the question "To whom do you belong?" The way people thought, acted and viewed themselves was tied to those with whom they shared life.

The third corner of the triangle is even more difficult for people today to grasp. Premoderns viewed themselves as being shaped by the land in which they lived. They were "place" people who were deeply rooted in a sense of physicality. This is not the case for most people today. We are "space" people who have a huge gulf lying between our physical and spiritual experiences. Therefore our personal identity is an abstract "mind" issue that supposedly remains constant regardless of where we live or with whom we share our life. In the ancient world, a person like Abraham defined himself by the God he worshiped, the people to whom he belonged and the land in which he lived. When God invited Abraham to leave his family and land, he encountered an identity crisis that would reshape everything he knew about himself and God. But God did not invite Abraham into an individualistic, "spiritual" experience. Instead, he promised to establish a new people and a new land through Abraham. God was establishing a new triangle.[7]

The same could be applied to the apostle Paul's identity. His encounter with Jesus on the road to Emmaus reframed his personal, vertical relationship with God, but his identity was also reshaped by people in the community—as Ananias prayed for Paul to be healed of blindness (Acts 9:17-19), Barnabas mentored him (Acts 9:27) and many others shared life with him. In addition, the gospel took concrete, physical form in local contexts. For instance, Paul's identity was shaped by the multicultural context of Antioch (Acts 11:19-30) and the leadership of the church there, as opposed to the context of the Jewish church in Jerusalem. As a result, Paul was the apostle to the Gentiles because he was shaped by a God at work in the context of the Gentiles.

As we think about how we shape our identity so that we break from the idols of the four Ps, we could adjust this triangle in this way (see fig. 7.2). We are shaped by the gospel as we participate with others in the church in a unique context.[8]

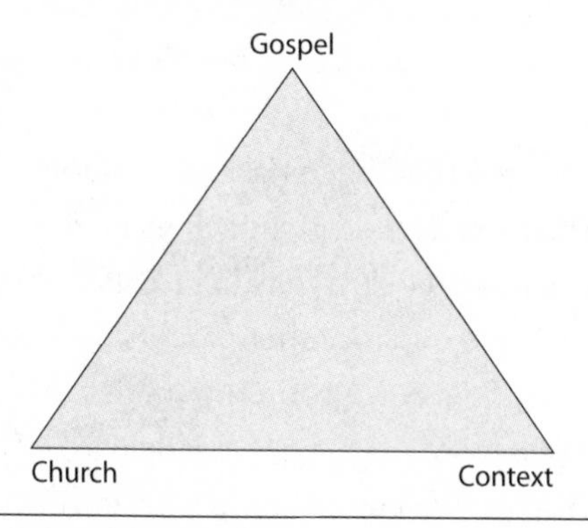

Figure 7.2. How we shape our identity

The truth of the gospel reshapes our identity relationally and through local contexts. A nutshell version of the gospel—the good news—could be stated as, "Jesus rose from the dead." The resurrection is a sign that the new life found in God's end times, when all of creation is restored, has broken backward into our present situation. The way we enter this reality is to experience life with others in our local situations, because resurrection life is at work in the entire triangle.

In practical terms, the way we spend time with one another as the church shapes who we are. If church is something that happens only in formal meetings that we can schedule on the calendar, then that is the primary venue in which the gospel will reshape our lives. But that is very limited. Some of the most significant identity-shaping conversations I've ever had occurred over coffee, while laughing and playing games with friends, or while going for a walk. The gospel breaks into our hanging out and re-forms our souls without our even knowing it.

To take this even further, when we see how God works in our local contexts, we see how the gospel penetrates all of life, and this declutters our souls. God is at work on our streets, in the ways we spend our time, through our hobbies and at work. We don't need to create more "spiritual" stuff to add to our calendars. We do need to see how the gospel is at work all around us and then get involved in those situations.

In concrete terms, this means a high schooler's small group meets at the school on Thursday mornings before classes start. It means shift workers meet at an all-night coffee shop at 3:00 a.m. A hockey dad leads a group for other parents on Sunday mornings before kids get on the ice. A group of families meets in the park where their kids can play.

Context is crucial. We can observe where we are already connected and organize our group life around that. We have to break the pattern of adding groups and commitments on top of everything else.

DECLUTTERING TIME IN THE REAL WORLD

When I was in my early twenties, I had a plan. I was committed to living a life that was not driven by the clock. Because I was time-conscious and I valued efficiency, I decided not to wear a watch—I found that I was constantly using it to measure how much I'd gotten done. I also committed to driving the speed limit, refused to over-extend myself and took a Sabbath every week, guarding this day of rest from needs and events that encroached. I was quite proud of myself—so much so that I couldn't understand why people who understood life so much better than I did were always in a hurry.

Well, my judgment of busy people has diminished since then. The school of life tends to change one's perspective a bit. When I was only responsible for me, I could say no to a lot of things. Now my life is rich with others who require things from me, and I find it much more difficult not to be hurried. (Four kids might have something to do with this.) Twenty years ago I was not pulled in a hundred different directions and being at rest came easily. Now the challenge is to find rest in the midst of this full life. I cannot just hang out with friends like I did once. I cannot just blow off my professional responsibilities like I blew off studying in college. The stakes—and the consequences—are much higher.

Our cluttered schedules are our reality. We fill our calendars with commitments and activities. Spouses pass one another coming and going. Kids have ball games, music practices and school functions. Then of course there is television. If there is an opening somewhere, we fill it.

At the same time, we cannot work seventy hours per week, volunteer for three committees, cart kids or grandkids all over town and expect to advance along the way of Jesus. We might be great managers of our calendars and have incredible capacity to juggle lots of activities, but the way of Jesus is not clutter-filled.

Often the clutter is not so much a result of having too much to do but a result of how we view the stuff that fills our calendars. Typically we treat every activity as having equal value. While we know that some things are more important than others, we tend to organize our days and weeks by a to-do list. And we don't consider what on that list is of greatest importance. In other words, we look at the "could-dos" and the "must-dos" the same way.

This is not about simplifying your life for the sake of simplicity. This is about finding out what's important to you and then focusing on that. It's about saying yes to those things that matter and investing your life in them.

FINDING THE MUST-DOS

In his book *The One Thing*, Gary Keller focuses not on the fact that we live crazy lives and need to simplify; rather, he invites people to think in terms of the "one thing."[9] Instead of making a list of activities and identifying which ones are most important, he proposes that we focus on the one thing that matters the most. What is the one thing at work that is going to move you in the direction of your goals? What is the one thing you can do to invest in your relationship with your spouse? What is the one thing you can do to be a better parent to your children? What is the one thing you can do to know God better? What is the one thing you can do to love people and lead the way relationally?

Keller suggests that we ask ourselves this question: What's the one thing I can do that will make everything else easier or unnecessary?

Think about it in terms of your job, to which you give eight hours per day: If you look at your list of fifty could-dos for this week, what are the ten that will have the most impact and move you furthest along toward your goals? Those are the should-dos. Of these should-dos, identify the one thing that matters the most. This is the must-do.

In my vocation, I have lots of plates spinning in my work with churches and other writers. Between calls to make, reports to write and contracts to send out, the list is long. As I look at my list, my "one thing" is the call to develop content for books that provide training and coaching for leaders. Doing this one thing—developing content—makes everything else easier or unnecessary. For instance, developing content is the part of my job that gives me the most energy. So when I focus on this one thing, whether I'm writing a book—as I'm doing now—working with a pastor in preparing an onsite consultation or training, or working with other writers, I get more done in less time.

Knowing this, I can move from allowing a long list of could-dos to dictate my day and collapsing into bed at night with unfinished tasks rolling around in my head—which causes stress, by the way—to focusing on what really matters in such a way that I get those things done.

You can apply the "one thing" approach to your small group as well. It shouldn't be difficult to produce a long list of could-dos for the group. From this, you might identify things that you should do each week. But what is the must-do one thing to which your group is called? What is the one thing that your group can do to:

- Commune with God more?
- Relate to one another in love?
- Engage your neighbors and networks?

Most of the time, we identify the one thing by observing what God is already doing through the group or individuals within the group.

Imagine this: a group of guys regularly eats at an ethnic restaurant for lunch at least once per week. They get to know the owners and talk with the workers on regular basis. The restaurant has a back room where they can have a bit of privacy. So they decide to begin a small group that meets over lunch. They plan to eat at the restaurant twice per week, one of these meals being a time when they talk about the Scriptures and pray for one another. In addition, they decide to adopt this restaurant as their place of mission. They want their group to be a public foretaste of what the kingdom of God might be. This is their one thing. They don't even have to do anything that different from what they're already doing. They focus on this one thing and see how God is at work in it.

A group's one thing is often related to what members enjoy doing. If people like playing board games, how could that be used to shape the group? (No one said fun couldn't be part of group life.) If some in the group have kids in the same activities, how can they creatively take advantage of those times together? If a member of the group is a sponsor in Big Brothers or Big Sisters, how might the group work together to be a blessing to the child?

FOCUSING ON THE MUST-DO

It's not enough for us to identify our must-do. We also have to learn to focus on it. In my work, this means carving out extended time that is solely devoted to my one thing. As opposed to dividing up my workday by going back and forth between all the items on my could-do list, focusing on the must-do gives me the space to make progress toward my goal. So every day I focus on my must-do, carving out extended time (two to four hours) to focus on that one thing. Then I group the other should-dos together to address at other points of my day.

This is the challenge in our modern culture. The craziness of our world barrages us with distractions. For instance, I could slip over to my email inbox or jump on Facebook or make a phone call right now. These activities all have value. But they can also distract me from focusing on my one thing. When I do this, I end up stressed at the end of the day because I haven't done what I feel I've been put on earth to do.

As a result, I don't have as much energy for the people in my life. My soul is stressed by the fact that I have not focused on what I'm called to do in my vocation. I don't have energy or space to hang out and just be with people; therefore I cannot focus on them. On the other hand, when I do spend the right amount of time focusing on my one thing, I have more energy for my family, friends in my small group and people in my neighborhood because I'm not thinking about all the stuff I have to get done. Instead of clutter, I can focus on people. My soul has space to listen, engage and share the richness of God's grace.

Keller suggests that if your one thing is part of your eight-hours-per-day vocational work, then block out four hours for it every day. Use the balance of your time to address everything else. Don't try to split your attention among too many things. When you do, you're much more likely to bring work home, which steals from your marriage, your home, your friends, your small group and the joy of hanging out.

Doing your one thing well involves focus. When you're leading your group, focus on the group. When you're at work, focus on work. When you're having lunch with a friend, focus on your friend. In our culture where everyone interrupts everyone else, develop the ability to sustain your attention on what is before you. Instead of doing a little outreach here and some humanitarian work there and some volunteer work at yet another place—trying to minister to everyone equally—focus on the people and places where God is clearly directing your attention. (More on this in chapter eight.)

FINISHING THE MUST-DO

Focus gives us the ability to pay attention right now to that which matters most. But focus alone will only get us halfway to our must-do. We also have to finish. In my work, I can focus on my writing for four hours straight every day. I can write a little on this chapter and then a little on the next. But I have to finish each step along the way in order for my must-do to matter.

Life is a journey, not a destination, a point I've made quite often in this book. And on a journey we take steps one at a time. We cannot take partial steps. We have to finish each small must-do that requires our focus right now.

When you're leading your group, many needs and issues will come to your attention. You'll see them in the lives of the group members and in your neighborhood and in the ministries to which the group feels called. Almost all of them are far bigger than what can be addressed at any one point in time. The key is to focus on the small must-do and then finish it. Often we engage people like a hummingbird, a little here, a little there. If people don't respond positively to us the first time, we move on. But repetition is the key. Faithful presence is essential to embodying and sharing the good news. Seeing that we need to finish the one thing gives us permission to "hang out"—to waste time with others in a way that people can see how we live and take steps on the way of Jesus with us.

Finishing the must-do that God gives us is rooted in the fact that the work of God's life is finished. Finishing is not so much about our completing the work as if the results depended on our action. It's about staying put and refusing to flit about—thereby adding more clutter—and trusting that God has already finished the work of the kingdom. The future promises of God are fulfilled, even though we don't see them as such yet. We finish because we trust, not because we have to produce. And one of the most important ways we finish is to rest. We practice Sabbath. Often today Sabbath is primarily about going to church. And for volunteers in the church, this often means more work. But in the fourth commandment in Exodus 20, Sabbath is not primarily about worship but about rest, about stopping from work. It's about rebelling against the tyranny of doing more, producing more and getting more out of life. Walter Brueggeman comments, "Sabbath is a practical divestment so that neighborly engagement, rather than production and consumption, define our lives."[10] Sabbath trains our souls, in other words, to make room for one another.

There is a time to finish the work, whether it is completed or not. Sabbath is not about reaching a point of exhaustion from all the work and ministry we're doing and being forced to rest. It is an expression of faith that God has finished his work and we are not the ones who make it happen. We lead not because we have to make it happen. We lead through faith. We lead through trust. We lead through rest. And by doing so, we declare that God's creation does not depend on us. God is at work. God works ahead of us. And if God rested then we must learn God's ways. Brueggemann continues, "YHWH is a Sabbath-keeping God, which fact ensures that restfulness and not restlessness is at the center of life. . . . Sabbath becomes a decisive, concrete, visible way of opting for and aligning with the God of rest."[11]

Sabbath gives us space to refrain from producing and to receive God's promises. It's about enjoying the reality that God is present and that others are present. We can then hang out with God and with others. Our souls can be open to one another because we can trust that God is moving like a grand river, and we are riding his flow whether we swim or not.

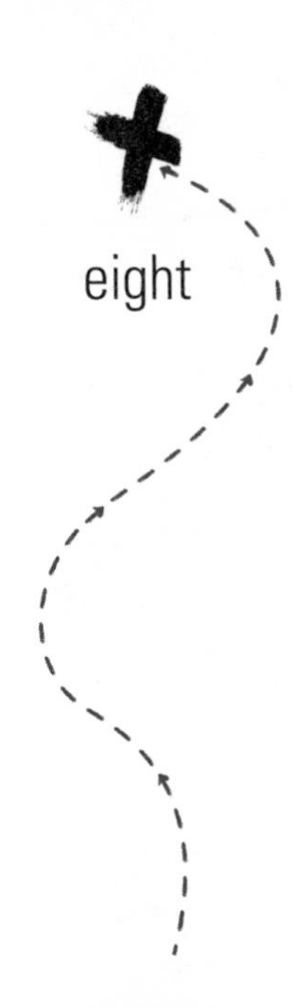

Make a Difference

The Sixth Practice

When I was visiting a church in Louisiana, the youth pastor told me about a girl named Jennifer, the daughter of a local gang leader. Some young people in one of the small groups had told Jennifer about Jesus and she had become a disciple. In fact, she had become a radical disciple. However, there was a problem. Jennifer's father told her she could believe whatever she wanted, but she could not go inside that church building. Luckily, the youth small group met on the school campus in the morning before classes started.

That group was Jennifer's tether, her family during a time of great turmoil. As she walked with Jesus that year, she realized she needed to forgive her abusive former boyfriend—who was now on death row. She visited him in jail and told him about Jesus. He became a disciple and led twenty-six other prisoners to Jesus before his sentence was carried out.

Over the course of that year, Jennifer's gang-leader dad saw the change in his daughter and relented. He told her she could go to whatever Christian meetings she wanted to. He did not realize she was already doing this because the meetings did not fit his expectations.

This group made a difference, one they did not expect. Many small groups aim at this, even to the point of organizing outreach, making prayer lists of friends who don't know Jesus, and investing in social justice programs. But most find it hard to get beyond the good intentions.

As many admit—and some are afraid to confess—it seems to me that Christians and non-Christians alike share a common disdain for things like evangelism and outreach programs. Christians feel pressured to do it as part of their duty and non-Christians want to run when we come their way. We know we are called to make a difference in our world—and I've yet to find a Christian who is unhappy with the fact that someone "evangelized" them—but we need to rethink how we "go and make disciples" (Matthew 28:19). We need ways of manifesting the way of Jesus so that people can see how we live in love, which gives us the right to talk about the way of Jesus.

This calls for a shift from doing outreach activities to living into a way that naturally and organically creates space for the proclamation of the gospel. We need a way of *being* difference makers as opposed to *doing* evangelism and social justice actions.

BEING VERSUS DOING

Mother Teresa once stated, "There are no great acts, only small things done with great love." Making a difference begins when we think in terms of being and not just doing. Too often we are tempted to make the mission of God in our world about activism, doing things to set the world right, whether through evangelism or social justice initiatives. We turn God's mission into a cause that we attack because we're trying to be obedient. While our motives might be good, focusing on actions will cause us to deviate from the way of

Jesus. It's one thing to do some activities now and then that look loving. It's another thing to be formed into the kind of person who loves. In the first instance we do things to be effective and maybe even to get credit for making a difference. In the second we love because we have been formed by the God of love and as a result love flows out of us.

The history of the early church illustrates this point. Its incredible growth within the Roman Empire changed world history. The church grew from three or four hundred followers of Jesus after the resurrection to more than thirty million people three centuries later. Many writers and speakers have challenged the church to get back to the methodology of the early church so that we can reproduce those results. Rarely, though, do they mention the need to get back to the way the people in those churches made a difference in their world.

Rodney Stark, an academic sociologist, studied the early church in its first three hundred years of life to see if he could unearth some previously missed reasons for its unprecedented growth. While his research led to many important insights, one specifically speaks to the church's way of life. History tells us that the Roman Empire was hit by widespread disease multiple times, which wiped out thousands of people. Roman citizens who had the means would flee the towns and cities hit by disease. Those without financial resources would quarantine infected family members, waiting for them to die. But records tell us that Christians would care for those who were ill, even nonbelievers abandoned to die, and survival rates were higher for those given care and nourishment. Many of those left to suffer and die became believers because Christians cared for them while putting their own lives at risk. There were no great acts, just small things done with great love. Because Christians loved over a period of time, in the same places with the same people, the world was changed.[1]

People don't love like this because it's the right thing to do. They don't love like this because they want their small group to grow or because they want their church to make a mark in history. They love like this because their being has been shaped by love. This is the work of the Spirit within us.

The kind of difference we make is connected to our identity. It flows out of who we are, not just what we do. Doing stuff to make a difference does not necessarily mean we are being difference makers. There is a difference between doing stuff and doing stuff that flows out of our being. While table 8.1 overemphasizes the contrast, it illustrates the centrality of *being* over *doing.*

Table 8.1. Being versus doing

	Being	Doing
Focus of mission	Group life	Outreach activities
Source of mission	Overflow	Effort
Goal of mission	Be a blessing	Add people to group
Power of mission	Love	Action
Key trait of mission	Conversations	Presentations

Being a difference maker includes doing things, but when we emphasize the doing we don't always experience the transformation of our being. God is at work in our world. God is making a difference, charting a path to make all things new. Our job is not to make the difference happen. Our job is to allow ourselves to be drawn into the difference that God is already making. As we do this, we move beyond activity and into a transformation of our being (Romans 12:1-2).

AN UNEXPECTED INSIGHT

I've found that answers to important questions come from unexpected places. While teaching a class on spiritual formation, I discovered a new way to talk about making a difference. This class was shaped by the ancient practice of Scripture reading called *lectio divina.* As opposed to reading the Bible in a way that's analytical (asking, "What does this mean?"), practical ("What do I do with this?") or inspirational ("What does this mean for my life?"), *lectio divina* invites the reader to enter into the imagination of the Scripture. Eugene Peterson writes:

> *Lectio divina* is a way of reading the Scriptures that is congruent with the way the Scriptures serve the Christian community as a witness to God's revelation of himself to us. It is the wise guidance developed through the centuries of devout Bible reading to discipline us, the readers of Scripture, into appropriate ways of understanding and receiving this text so that it is formative for the way we live our lives, not merely making an impression on our minds or feelings. It intends the reading of Scripture to be a permeation of our lives by the revelation of God.[2]

In other words, this approach to reading Scripture gets the way of being found within the words into our being. There are four basic parts to the process, involving four readings of the same passage. Here's an example of how you might lead a group or proceed yourself through *lectio divina*:

- ***Read: Prepare yourself to hear God's Word.*** When you read the words the first time, pay attention to what's being said in a broad way. Make yourself comfortable and open yourself to God. Pay attention to the words you hear. What stands out to you? Notice any thoughts, pictures, memories or experiences that arise in your imagination. After you read, sit in silence and allow the words to resonate within you.
- ***Reflect: Meditate on what stood out to you.*** When preparing to read the passage a second time, give yourself permission to reflect on the words. What thoughts naturally arise? What's the

response of your heart? After reading, sit in silence and roll over the words, thoughts and feelings inside you.

- ***Respond: Offer your thoughts, emotions and sensations back to God.*** With this third reading, let the words of the text enter into your imagination in such a way that they prompt some kind of response. Let the ways that the reading has touched your heart and mind spawn a prayer or emotion back to God. Let what is in you be expressed, whatever it may be.
- ***Remain: Wait before God in his presence.*** With this final reading, allow yourself to sit with the words as if you are sitting with a best friend. Then imagine that you are sitting in stillness with God. Rest in God and be with God. Is something emerging from this time with God that you sense you need to try out? What action steps or experiments might be called for?[3]

As I have reflected on the people who have made a difference in my life, I have seen that they ministered to me through these same four steps. They paid attention to my needs. Then they reflected and listened to the Lord because they did not presume to know what I needed. At this point they responded; they acted in concrete ways. Then at last they established a pattern of remaining—they lived out a faithful presence.

Just as the four parts of *lectio divina* invite us to enter into the imagination of God's Word so that its truth can enter into us, so the four parts can help us enter into our local situations in a way that we do small acts with great love with the same people over time in the same place.

At the end of Colossians, Paul's words correlate with the four parts of *lectio divina*:

> Devote yourselves to prayer, being watchful and thankful. And pray for us, too, that God may open a door for our

> message, so that we may proclaim the mystery of Christ, for which I am in chains. Pray that I may proclaim it clearly, as I should. Be wise in the way you act toward outsiders; make the most of every opportunity. Let your conversation be always full of grace, seasoned with salt, so that you may know how to answer everyone. (Colossians 4:2-6)

In this passage, the steps are: (1) be watchful and thankful, (2) pray that God may open a door, (3) pray that I may proclaim, and (4) act toward outsiders with wisdom. Table 8.2 puts it all together.

Table 8.2. *Lectio divina* and Colossians 4:2-6

Step	*Lectio divina*	Colossians 4:2-6	Difference making
1.	Read	Be watchful and thankful.	Pay attention to neighborhoods and networks.
2.	Reflect	Pray that God may open a door.	Reflect in order to understand.
3.	Respond	Pray that I may proclaim.	Act in the local.
4.	Remain	Act toward outsiders with wisdom.	Be a faithful presence.

Let's think through these four steps in the context of group life.

STEP 1: PAY ATTENTION TO NEIGHBORHOODS AND NETWORKS

Be watchful and thankful (Colossians 4:2).

In David Benner's book *Opening to God*, he calls the first step of *lectio divina* "attending." He challenges readers to develop the discipline of paying attention not only to the Scriptures but also to what is going on in life around us. He invites us to read life, to read ourselves and to read creation. He calls us to wake up to what is already present but we often miss.

When we develop the practice of paying attention, we learn to read God's creation to see where he is already on mission. We learn to read not only what's going on inside of us, but also to read what is happening in other people. We learn needs, yearnings and hopes. We read the story of neighborhoods, of family members. We read stories that lack good news. And we read where people are hoping to find good news.

To develop the practice of paying attention to life and to our neighborhoods, we must heed Benner's counsel: "Prayerful paying attention is not scrunching up our willpower and tightening our focus, but simply opening our self to what we encounter. This makes it much more an act of release than effort."[4] When we pay attention when we are reading a good novel, we let the story unfold. We don't work to make it happen. We let it be and we learn to attend to what's going on. This is what we do when we attend to the world around us. We observe. We listen. We ask questions. We give it time to sink in.

In my book *Difference Makers,* I talk about two sets of relationships where we can make a difference. The first is neighbors and the second is networks, which might include relatives, work connections, club memberships and the like. I then encourage readers to draw a tic-tac-toe box for each (see fig. 8.1). For the one marked "Neighbors," write your name in the middle square and the names of those who live around you in the eight other squares. For "Networks," write the names of those closest to you in your various networks of relating.[5]

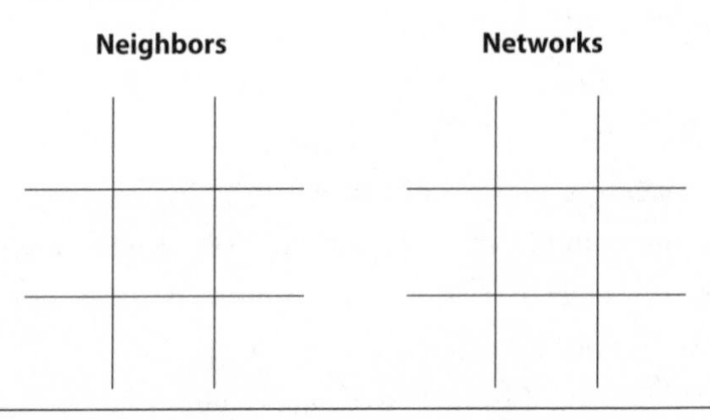

Figure 8.1. Two sets of relationships

The names you listed above are not based on preference. Søren Kierkegaard wrote, "The neighbor is the person who is nearer to you than anyone else, yet not in the sense of preferential love, since to love someone who in the sense of preferential love is nearer than anyone else is self-love—'do not the pagans also do the same?' The neighbor, then, is nearer to you than anyone else. . . . 'The neighbor' is what thinkers call 'the other,' that by which the selfishness in self-love is to be tested."[6]

Kierkegaard is challenging the romantic notions of spontaneous and preferential love as spoken of by the poets. This can be erotic love or friendship love, but poetic love is always preferential. We have eros out of preference. We have friends because we prefer one person over the other. Kierkegaard continues, "Erotic love and friendship are the very peak of self-esteem, the I intoxicated with the other I."[7] These spontaneous loves can ebb and flow with the whims of our nature: "Spontaneous love can be changed from itself, it can be changed over the years, as is frequently enough seen."[8] In other words, we love as long as it is pleasing to do so. But is that love?

When we love our neighbor or those in our networks, it is not out of preference. We don't choose them. They're just there. They might be enemies who repulse us. They might be nobodies we could easily ignore. They might be strangers with whom we share nothing in common. But they are near us. And by loving a neighbor we love the entire world. Kierkegaard writes, "If a person loves the neighbor in one single other human being, he then loves all people."[9]

STEP 2: REFLECT IN ORDER TO UNDERSTAND

Pray that God may open a door (Colossians 4:3).

On the heels of paying attention, we ponder, reflect, meditate and pray. We listen to God, to what the Spirit is already doing and to what Jesus is calling us to do. We don't jump to conclusions. We ask a few questions: What needs do I see? What are the gifts I have to meet those needs? What is God already doing? What does God want to do?

Too often we assume we know what people need. Usually this falls into one of two assumptions: (1) people need to hear the gospel message so they'll become Christians like us and join our church, or (2) people need our help in a physical way so they can live like we do.

While I was leading a small group a few years ago, my pastor challenged all the groups to do at least one outreach activity per month. So one month we'd play volleyball at an apartment complex. The next we'd throw a cookout for some friends. The next we'd do some kind of service project. The goal was to develop friends so we could lead them to Christ. This approach was based on research showing that the majority of faithful followers of Jesus were led to the Lord by a friend, family member, coworker or neighbor. In fact, the statistics on this are staggeringly high—some sources say that more than ninety percent of believers came to Christ this way. While stranger evangelism can be effective and conversion experiences involving mass events or multimedia presentations can be effective at the point of decision, relationships influence people the most when they're considering whether they want to follow Jesus.

The logical conclusion then is to train Christians in relationship evangelism. Relationships are more effective than things like door-to-door witnessing, handing out tracts or organizing evangelistic rallies. And there are some great techniques that facilitate relationship evangelism. For instance, hang a poster group members can use to list friends and neighbors for whom they want to pray. These names could come from the two tic-tac-toe diagrams above.

Additional technical strategies might include:

- Identify three to five people on this list who seem to be most open to the gospel.
- Pray for these people as individuals.
- Pray together as a group.

- Develop relationships on the relationship.
- Do fun things together with those people.

These fun things are often called "Matthew parties" because Jesus began his relationship with Matthew by going to a party that included religious outcasts. The goal is the create a nonreligious environment where Christians can naturally rub shoulders with those who don't know Jesus.

At the same time, we need to go beyond techniques. If we don't, we can easily turn relationship evangelism into loving non-Christians only because we want them to become one of us. And this is not love at all. In fact, Andrew Root in his book *The Relational Pastor* challenges the whole idea of "friendship evangelism":

> So-called friendship evangelism does not love the person; the love of person has no ends, it only acts so that the beloved can live and love. Friendship evangelism actually loves the idea, the third thing it is trying to get people to know, do or come to. In friendship evangelism I don't really love the person, but the idea of church membership, the idea of converting you. I love not you but the thing I'm using the relationship to get you to do.[10]

At first you might respond, "Isn't it loving to point my friend to the gospel since Jesus is the only one who can help her 'live and love'?" However, Root is not challenging the reality that the gospel most easily spreads across relational lines. Nor is he saying that abundant life is not found in Jesus. Rather, he's pointing out the fact that if we are going to have loving relationships, we need to relate to neighbors, coworkers, family members and friends in a such a way that we encounter them in the relationship instead of using the relationship to get something from them. Love does not mean we peddle the gospel so another person will become one of us. It means we love. We engage. We listen in order to understand the person's needs instead of going forth with a preconceived notion of those needs.

This also applies to social justice initiatives. Love means we relate to those in need in such a way that we actually listen to them. We don't influence them to become more like us. Root states, "Friendship can have no goal of influence—it seeks only to share our place, to invite us to share in the life of the other."[11] We befriend in order to love neighbors and those in our networks because we are created to give and receive love.

Love is love only when it is the end, not a means to the end of getting people saved and into our churches. It's not a means to change the lives of those in need or deal with social injustice. Love calls us to see people, to enter into dialogue, to embrace the fact that the other might affect us as we affect them.

This was made ever so clear to me when I sat in a small group with a man who had grown up in generational poverty, spent quite a bit of time in jail and afterward lived in what we would consider a low-income neighborhood. He proclaimed, "Don't send your money down here. If you want to get to know us, you are more than welcome. But we don't want to be like you."

When we listen, we attain understanding and we see how God might be moving in new ways. Ultimately this means we listen in prayer as we listen to real needs. God wants to speak to us about how the Spirit is moving and how we can get involved.

STEP 3: ACT IN THE LOCAL

Proclaim clearly (Colossians 4:4).

At this point we act. We respond to the need. When we think about what it means to make a difference, we usually think in terms of the actions we take. However, appropriate action comes only after we take time to pay attention and reflect. In the book *Mission in the 21st Century,* the authors identify five primary ways our action plays out:[12]

1. Proclaiming the good news of the kingdom, that the God who rose Jesus from the dead is here to redeem all.
2. Teaching, baptizing and nurturing new believers in the reality that we no longer need to put up with that which entraps us and can be set free by the power of God's Spirit.
3. Responding to human need in loving service, offering a new way of living by serving those who have little (or nothing) to offer in return.
4. Seeking to transform unjust structures of society to demonstrate that God can change a culture or a local situation in ways that allow people to experience his peace and wholeness.
5. Striving to safeguard the integrity of creation and sustain and renew the life of the earth, because God's creation is good.

How we act in our local contexts will vary from place to place. There is no one-size-fits-all missional approach. We act in a way that resembles improvisation more than the memorization of lines. As we pay attention and reflect, we enter the ways of love and we risk. We go forth to be a blessing in unexpected ways. This is the power of Jennifer's story recounted at the beginning of this chapter. Here are a few principles that can empower loving improvisation:

- Respond to the needs you observe. Maybe it's a single mother who needs assistance or a family who cannot buy food because of job loss. It could be that the neighborhood is disconnected and you want to host a picnic or there's a need for tutoring at the local school.
- Do it with others. Jesus never sent people out alone. The apostle Paul always ministered as part of a team.

- Learn to share your three-minute testimony with one another in the group. Take an evening to write it out and practice telling the three basic parts: your life before knowing Christ, how you encountered Christ for the first time and how Christ has changed your life.
- When a person comes to faith in Christ, ask them to make a list of five neighbors or people in their networks. Help them share their testimony with those five people within a week. This is a great first step in their discipleship journey.

STEP 4: BE A FAITHFUL PRESENCE

"Be wise in the way that you act toward outsiders; make the most of every opportunity. Let your conversation be always full of grace, seasoned with salt, so that you may know how to answer everyone" (Colossians 4:5-6).

To make a difference, we must learn to remain, to develop life patterns of being present in the community, living out the reality of what it means to be God's people. We must learn to put the beauty of God, his self-sacrificial love, on display in a repetitious way that facilitates life and transforms neighborhoods, families and workplaces.

Faithful presence means we put the life of God in our midst on display so that others can see God's life in us. The problem is that most of the time in our small groups we divide our life into the part that's for group insiders and the part that's for outsiders. For instance, prayer, worship and Bible teaching are for insiders. Service projects and evangelism are what insiders do for outsiders. But this is an artificial division, one that does not fully demonstrate God's life in us.

Imagine that you were a part of Paul's entourage in the first century as he began ministering in Ephesus. Pull out a study Bible and look at a map of Ephesus. It was a large city for the time but small in size, only about four miles long and two miles wide. The houses were built right next to one another. They didn't have private garages or glass windows. Nor did they have big yards and fences to separate their homes. The reality is that multiple generations of one family would share one roof or a series of connected homes. It was a different world.

As you and the rest of Paul's team start to minister in this city, all kinds of God things happen. Someone gets healed. Someone is set free from a demon. A family converts to be Jesus followers. People in the synagogue ask questions. Soon you start meeting in someone's home to talk about Jesus, worship God, eat together and pray. The New Testament called this church.

Most people in Ephesus, and everyone in that section of the city, would have known about Paul and this little group that had been meeting to worship a crucified Jewish Messiah. Why? Because the group had no choice but to be present in their neighborhood—it was how local architecture worked at the time. Everything the believers did was public. Anyone could see how they lived as Christians. People could observe the way they prayed and worshiped simply by walking by the host's home. Christians' self-sacrifice and love were on display every day. There was no division between private spiritual activities for church insiders and public ministry activities for outsiders. The kind of division that puts prayer and community into the category of insider ministry and evangelism and social justice into the category of outsider ministry is a relatively new idea in the history of the church.

Since we don't live in first-century Ephesus, we must develop ways of living in our neighborhoods that demonstrate who we are as followers of Jesus to outsiders. Three things rise to the top of the list:

- ***Offer hospitality.*** Invite a neighbor or a friend to a simple meal and share common conversation about life. Pay attention, reflect on what you hear and act on what you sense God leading you to do. Do this on a monthly basis, either with the same family or with a few others. Try to focus on a small number of people so you can invest in them.

- ***Display generosity.*** Pay attention to the needs you see. Invest your time, resources and emotional energy as God opens doors.
- ***Proclaim forgiveness.*** Announce the forgiveness of God. Talk about how God has loved you when you did not deserve it and how this love is available to all.

GROWING IN DIFFERENCE MAKING

When the Spirit of God comes to reside in us, we will naturally desire to make a difference. But for most people, it's only a difference-making seed that lies within, one that never realizes its potential. Even though they try a few things, this seed never grows to the point of having an effect for a variety of reasons. Often, people get discouraged by initial resistance or even overt failure. They just don't see the results that they expected.

The truth is that we all start out as novices in difference making. We begin the pattern of paying attention, reflecting, acting and being a faithful presence with expectations of seeing God move through us, but the reality is that we might not know how to do it very well. It's a process that we learn by doing, and as we do it our capacity to make a difference grows.

So the effect at the beginning might look insignificant. But as we practice this pattern of making a difference and continue practicing it through repetition, we will grow in our ability to express God's love for our neighbors and those in our networks. Over time, if we keep at it, our ability to engage our context with the gospel might grow like this.

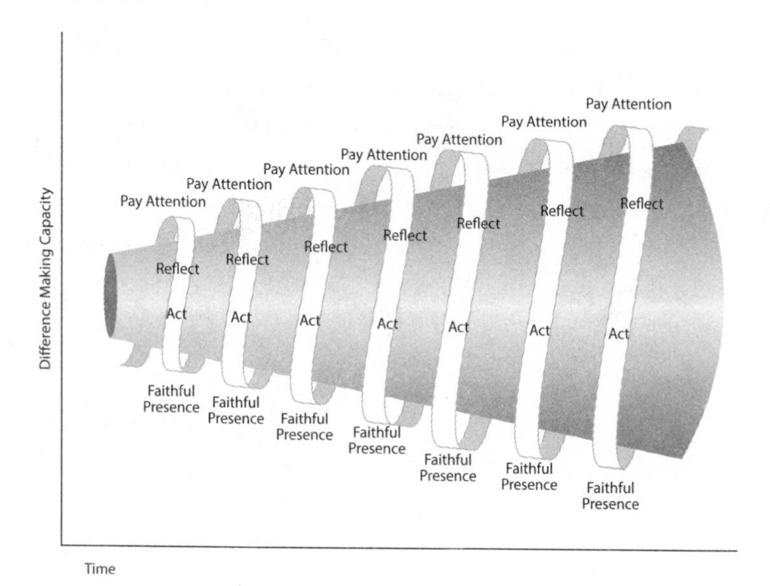

Figure 8.2. Making a difference over time

We don't do this because we're promised success. We enter on this path because it is the way of following Jesus into the world. It's the way of participating in what God is doing to redeem all of creation. Yet if we keep at it, we will be effective in sharing the gospel. The key is faithful repetition—loving because God has called us to love.

Eric Lerew, a leader in Chicago, wrote recently about faithful presence in a Facebook post:

> I love what God is doing in my neighborhood! On my way to the mailbox I ran into the guy that lives next door. His wife has joined our group for a meal a few times and he and I have talked about connecting. This morning he was heading out for his daily walk around the block so I decided to join him. About halfway around the block we stopped just to talk. One thing led to another and we ended up praying for each other.

I felt the tangible presence of God as we invited Jesus to work in our lives. God touched my heart in major way as he prayed for me. As we walked and talked we decided we would each read the Gospel of Mark and talk about what we're reading the next time we see each other. I've been praying for God's kingdom to come in my neighborhood and today I experienced the answer to my prayer.[13]

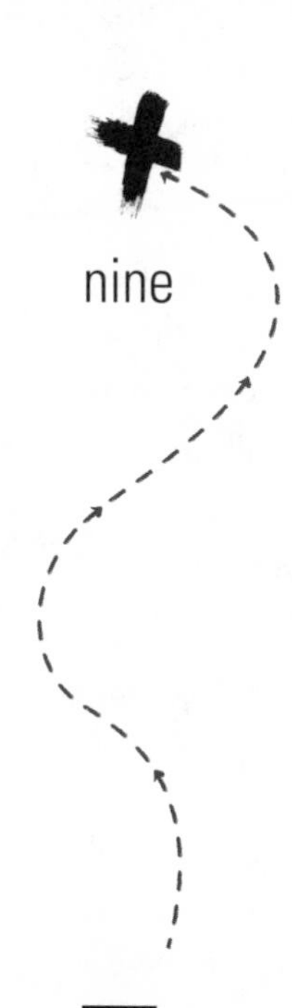

nine

Fight Well

The Seventh Practice

The real world we traverse outside our church activities is full of conflict, adventure and violence. Fighting happens at all levels: globally as nations go to war, nationally as politicians tear each other apart, and locally as neighbors let petty differences cloud their judgment.

It also happens in the church. And in small groups. We wish we could lead our groups without having to deal with such adventures, but, alas, conflict comes with people. Being human comes with differences and differences lead to conflict.

Of course, every small group leader training manual or book says as much. Some call it conflict. Others call it "storming." M. Scott Peck calls it chaos.[1] When people get to know one another, someone is bound to cause offense. Sometimes it's as minor as a huff after an innocent comment is taken the wrong way. Sometimes it's as major as a yelling match. A few years ago a small group leader asked to meet with me. He told me that while I had been out of town over the weekend, his coleader and another group member had almost gotten in a fistfight after church on Sunday. Larry Crabb writes,

"Conflicts arise when people have opposing agendas, competing agendas where something deeply personal is at stake."[2]

Few small groups deal with conflict well. Some get out their boxing gloves and duke it out. Some run away emotionally so they don't have to deal with the real issues. Some run away literally as they seek out another group or quit small groups all together. A lot pretend the conflict is not there and simply coexist in what Peck calls "pseudocommunity."

The way of Jesus requires us to learn to fight well. While the group leader might have received some training on conflict and been forewarned that it would happen, that's not enough to deal with conflict in the group when it happens. And the time for the whole group to learn is not when it's swept up in conflict. I've never seen a group in the midst of heated emotions learn how to handle conflict effectively. It's too late at that point.

Miroslav Volf writes, "In the light of Christ's self-sacrifice and resurrection, the future belongs to those who give themselves in love, not to those who nail others to a cross."[3] The future of every group depends on whether group members respond to conflict in love or in anti-love. Fighting will happen. How you respond to that fight is the question. We must be willing to get in the ring and learn how to fight well.

THE REALITY OF CONFLICT

Jesus talked about conflict in terms of having enemies. He taught:

> But to you who are listening I say: Love your enemies, do good to those who hate you, bless those who curse you, pray for those who mistreat you. If someone slaps you on one cheek, turn the other also. If someone takes your coat, do not withhold your shirt. Give to everyone who asks you, and if anyone takes what belongs to you, do not demand it back. Do to others as you would have them do to you.

> If you love those who love you, what credit is that to you? Even sinners love those who love them. And if you do good to those who are good to you, what credit is that to you? Even sinners do that. And if you lend to those from whom you expect repayment, what credit is that to you? Even sinners lend to sinners, expecting to be repaid in full. But love your enemies, do good to them, and lend to them without expecting to get anything back. Then your reward will be great, and you will be children of the Most High, because he is kind to the ungrateful and wicked. Be merciful, just as your Father is merciful. (Luke 6:27-36)

Little disrupts our life like an enemy. But most of the time when we think of enemies, we think of terrorists who threaten our country, managers who are announcing layoffs or thieves who threaten the safety of our family. We think of enemies as those who cause us harm but whom we don't really know personally. These are distant enemies.

What about the up-close-and-personal enemy? Your spouse can mistreat you. Your coworker can lie to get the commission you deserve. Your friend can decide she doesn't have time for you anymore. Your kids can stop listening to you.

And, of course, enemies can show up in your small group. Kim has unrealistic expectations of Terri and both get frustrated. Tom annoys people with his platitudes and last week insulted Tracy for her lack of faith. Jerry has an annoying laugh that reminds Tammi of her abusive father. On and on and on it goes.

When enemies show up, our natural response is one of fight or flight. These are self-protective reactions based not on reason but arising from the instinctive part of our brain that responds to threat or danger. For instance, if you are walking along a trail in the woods and an animal jumps out ready to attack you, you don't have to think about your response. You will either run away or start swinging a stick. Any kind of threat can kick this fight-or-flight impulse into gear, and group conflict is no exception. When groups fight, members tend to react without thinking—blaming, judging and trying to fix one another. Fighting is when people attack each other directly. Flight occurs when they can't face conflict and run from the threat.

Of course, we don't have to allow this self-protection reflex to rule how we respond. We are not animals who are controlled by instinct. In his incredibly helpful book *Caring Enough to Confront*, David Augsburger writes about five options from which we can choose when we find ourselves in conflict:

1. ***"I'll get them."*** This is an I win/you lose scenario that puts the fight response into action. It's based on the assumption that one person is completely right and the other is completely wrong. In small groups this often plays out in indirect, passive-aggressive ways, with people sharing their perspective with everyone in the group—except for the person with whom they have conflict.

2. ***"I'll get out."*** In this situation, the flight reaction is carried out to its logical end. The conflict presents an apparently hopeless situation and one of the parties decides to remove himself or herself from the threat. In some cases, especially when abuse is involved, this is the only option. But in most small group situations, leaving usually means that everyone loses.

3. ***"I'll give in."*** This is another form of flight. One person yields to the other out of motivations that may range from feelings of unworthiness to wanting to keep the peace. While on the outside it might look like the conflict has subsided, the real issues have not been addressed. Most importantly, the soul of the person who gives in shrivels.

4. ***"I'll meet you halfway."*** At first glance this might look like a good way forward since no two people will ever agree on everything. But the reality is that meeting halfway means both parties have given in halfway. They are settling for two half-truths rather than dealing with what is real and allowing their souls to come out. As Augsburger notes, "Only when we care enough to tussle with the truth can we test, retest, refine and perhaps find more of it through our working at it seriously."[4]

5. ***"I care enough to allow my soul to manifest."*** Augsburger calls this the "I care enough to confront" option or the "I want relationship and I also want honest integrity" position. I broaden this in my application to group conflict because conflict is not always about confrontation. Conflict provides opportunities for our souls to come out from hiding. It creates a new space for us to discover what's real and what we need to be honest about. Direct confrontation of the other person is part of this soul manifestation option, but most often in a situation of conflict, we don't even know what's true until we begin the journey and allow our souls to come out.

The goal is to learn to fight with each other in a way that reflects option five. But most of us need training in order to do this well. And this training should come before the conflict occurs, not while it is occurring.

A few years ago, the kids in a small group I know of were playing downstairs while the adults met in the living room. During this playtime one child ended up with his legs tied together with duct tape. What to that point had been a great group took a sharp turn for the worse. Conflict did not just show up. It erupted. Some blamed. Others defended. Attack and withdrawal shifted back and forth like a game of tug of war. Somebody had to win and somebody had to lose. The leaders cried for help. Multiple pastors got involved.

Weeks of processing led to a lose-lose end. The group was just not prepared to deal with the reality of conflict.

We all make choices in the midst of conflict. But we are much more likely to make wise choices that are not driven by our fight-or-flight impulses if we are aware of the reality of conflict and prepare ourselves with some healthy ways of responding before we enter into it.

STAGES OF RELATIONSHIP DEVELOPMENT

The journey of the Jesus way in a group usually follows a predictable path of group development. It includes five stages: forming, storming, norming, performing and re-forming. Although these stages are described as linear in nature and are therefore somewhat artificial, they do help us see typical patterns of relationship development.

This process begins when people gather in superficial relationships, protecting their self-interests and questioning everything that happens. This is the forming stage of group development. At this stage, everything is new and exciting, but there are also many questions and apprehensions. People have high hopes for community and mission. They might know what these things mean in theory, but they don't really know what they mean in real life or this real situation.

After the group forms, it enters the storming, or conflict, stage. This is when people begin to see reality. They learn about each other, what they like and do not like. Sarah talks too much. Jeremy has an annoying laugh. John dominates. Ken lies sometimes. Group members also see things about themselves that God wants to change, and they question whether or not they want this to happen. Tom realizes that he rebels against authority. God shows Sandra that she is controlled by anger. John and Debbie learn just how bad their marriage really is. In some groups, this stage looks like chaos. In others, it is quiet discomfort with one another.

When people are willing to work through the storm and die to their personal self-interests, they enter into the norming stage. At this point members accept each other, work to meet each other's needs and support one another. The group has become family-like; it has found its identity because it has worked through the struggles of the storm. This is the stage when the group begins to experience the power of a community on mission.

Following norming is the performing stage, when the group focuses in earnest on being a community on mission. While the group may have begun with the call to mission clearly stated and even formed around a specific mission, after the group has normed, it is much more natural to move into ministry in the neighborhood.

The final stage of development is the re-forming stage. No group is perpetually the same. God leads groups into new ventures. A new team of leaders arises to start a new group or the group births a new group that will enter into God's mission in new ways.

The way can be impeded when group members move from the forming stage and begin to experience the storm. When people have previously been stuck in religious relationships where they did not deal with conflict, they may not be sure how to handle their emotions about the group, their thoughts about other people or the personality differences they experience. Many see storming as sinful. They operate from a perspective that keeps them in a middle zone—not too high and not too low—where they feel guilty when they have relational struggles. They balk at anything that looks like conflict and retreat into an emotional piety that keeps them distant. In many cases this involves hiding behind Bible study conversations. People fill the time with talk about what the Bible means, cross-referencing other Scriptures that are relevant to the topic and discussing theological ideas. We do this because it fits nicely into our comfort zone.

REVERTING BACK TO OUR COMFORT ZONE

A few years ago I was doing some work that reminded me of life on the farm. Even though I had not lived on a farm for more than twenty years, the feelings of familiarity flooded over me. I realized that I know farming. It's in my blood. I could walk on a farm today and start hauling hay, feeding cows and driving a tractor without any conscious thought. It's familiar. It's safe. And when I step out in a new direction vocationally, I often look back at the life of the farm and think, "Maybe I should go back. I know how to do that."

These reflections have caused me to think about how we move into the way of Jesus as groups. If you have participated in church life for very long at all, there are ways of doing church that have been woven into you, some good, some neutral and some negative. When a group encounters a new way of doing church, they might embrace the idea from a logical point of view, but that does not mean the new idea becomes part of the people. Nor does it mean that it becomes part of the leadership.

The old way, that which we leave behind for the sake of the new, remains a part of us. It is woven into us as something familiar. Neurologists tell us that these familiar ways have actually shaped how our brains work. When we introduce a change, we are fighting against how we've trained our brains to think. Imagine a rubber band wrapped around your two forefingers. The new idea is your right hand pulling away from the left, which represents the old familiar ways. The more the right hand pulls away, the more tension on the rubber band. The old ways of the left hand are anchored. They are safe. And they worked for us in the past—at least that's how we remember them when the tension rises. It takes a lot of tension to move the rooted ways of our familiar past.

When this tension arises we experience a form of conflict. For instance, when groups shift from a standard Bible study approach to meetings that are more focused on embodying the presence of

Christ (practice two), it's natural to feel like something is just not quite right. And if we are unaware of it, the fight-or-flight impulse will arise. When this occurs we want to get back to our comfort zone as quickly as possible. This pattern of reverting back to what we know is quite common. If we've depended on comfort food in the past, we'll toss aside our diet whenever stress hits us. I've seen it with small group leaders for years. Those who have been shaped by a Sunday school teacher imagination will start leading a conversational small group that is relational and life-giving. But as soon as someone difficult joins the group, the stress causes them to revert to being a Sunday school teacher so they can more easily control the meetings. We could illustrate it as in figure 9.1.

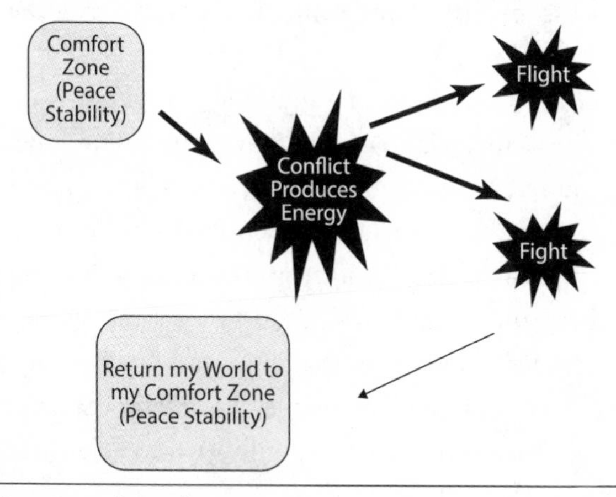

Figure 9.1. Reverting to the comfort zone

We see this clearly in the stories of the exodus. Even though the people of Israel had cried out for God's deliverance, when they experienced the unfamiliarity of wandering in the wilderness, they looked back on their life in Egypt and wished they could return. When problems that come with new ways of living arise, we naturally revert back the old ways for answers. It's normal. The old ways are woven into us.

To change this, we have to press through the tension instead of reverting back to the comfortable and familiar. Pressing forward leads us into the darkness of unknown, where we are without crutches. There we are forced to depend on God and allow the Spirit to train us in new ways of life.

EXPANDING OUR COMFORT ZONE

Instead of reverting back to the old comfort zone, we need to learn to see conflict as an opportunity to expand it. Without conflict we will remain within the comfort of what we already know. John Howard Yoder writes, "Conflict is socially useful; it forces us to attend to new data from new perspectives. It is useful in interpersonal process; by processing conflict, one learns skills, awareness, trust, and hope."[5]

Conflict creates tension that draws us out of our comfort zone and, if we press through it, our comfort zone will expand. As Alan Roxburgh notes, "The size of a comfort zone is an indicator of the degree to which you can discuss the differences of values, opinions, frameworks, beliefs, habits and attitudes between you and others."[6] If a comfort zone is small or limited to a certain set of beliefs or opinions, conflict can shatter that zone very easily. The larger the comfort zone with a group of people, the greater the ability to deal with conflict. However, usually the only way we expand our comfort zones is through conflict.

Let's return to the rhythms of the way of Jesus introduced in chapter three: communion, relating and engagement. We can intend to grow in each of these, even developing specific strategies and making concrete plans. We can implement those plans to the best of our abilities. However, every group experiences barriers that hinder us from living it out. Conflict provides opportunities to tear down those barriers. This can be illustrated with a sailing chart of sorts (see fig. 9.2).

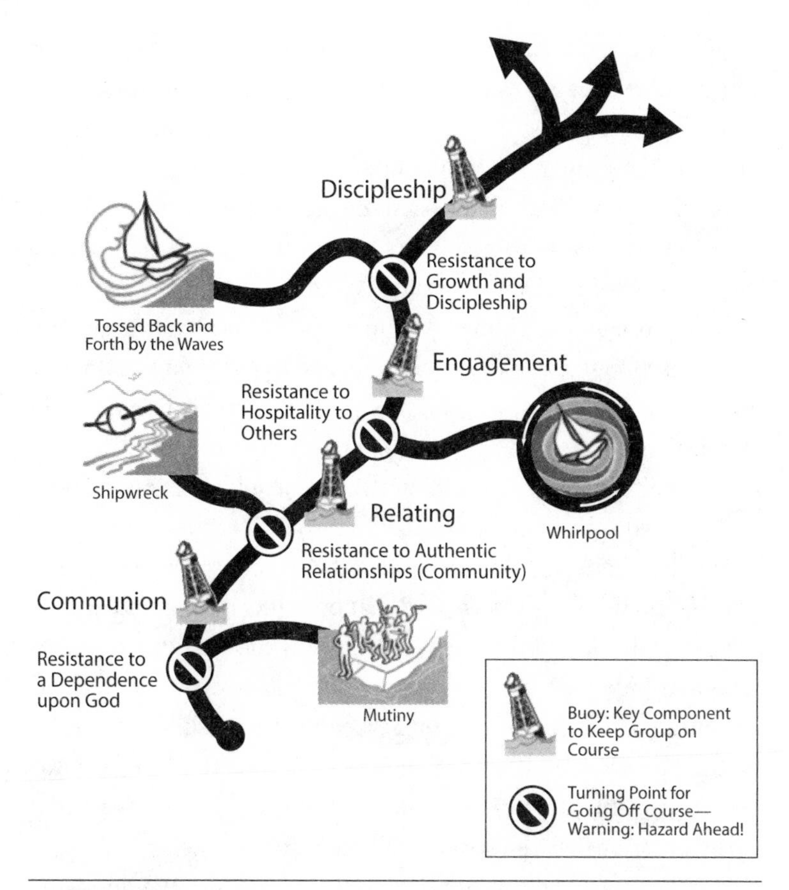

Figure 9.2. Moving past barriers

As we walk together, we will encounter the tendency to cling to our own ideas and thoughts about what the group should be. We are tempted to resist dependence on God, both as individuals and as a group. It's the conflict between what "I" want and what God wants to do through us. When we resist and hold on to that which is causing the conflict, we get off track and mutiny will occur at some point. Communion with God as a group is a gift that arrives as a blessing, not something we work up and make happen. It occurs as we let go and discover God together.

When we resist authentic relationships, groups shipwreck. But when groups create a safe place where people can trust each other and share their lives, they begin to experience relating. Here we find belonging and a sense of family.

Barriers arise in us as we try to engage our local communities. Showing hospitality to neighbors, coworkers, friends and family members will almost always result in conflict of some kind. We don't get to choose our neighbors. And many of them rub us wrong. We will want to walk away, to ignore them and to move on to someone else. When we do this, we enter a whirlpool of trying to hold on to people we like or reaching out to people who are like us. If we want to continue to experience community, we must learn to give it away. And we do this by being hospitable to those who cause conflict.

Finally, when we resist the conflict that comes through personal growth and discipleship, we find that both individuals and groups are tossed back and forth by the waves of life. We don't remain stagnant. Either we move forward and advance or we get pushed around by life. But when we embrace the discipleship that comes by the Spirit's formation and embrace the practices we need to grow up in Christ, we discover our new steps and receive answers to the questions of what God is calling us to.

Conflict creates opportunities for us to grow up. We don't like conflict, but we need it. The goal is to provide safe places for people to press through the tension so that they overcome the fight-or-flight impulse, achieve resolution and enter a new comfort zone. It might look like figure 9.3.

Here's the challenge for leaders: the goal is not to get others to expand their comfort zones so they line up with yours or to act the way you want them to. The goal is for you to own your response so you can expand your comfort zone and create space for others to join you in the process. We do this through a basic seven-step process of conflict resolution.

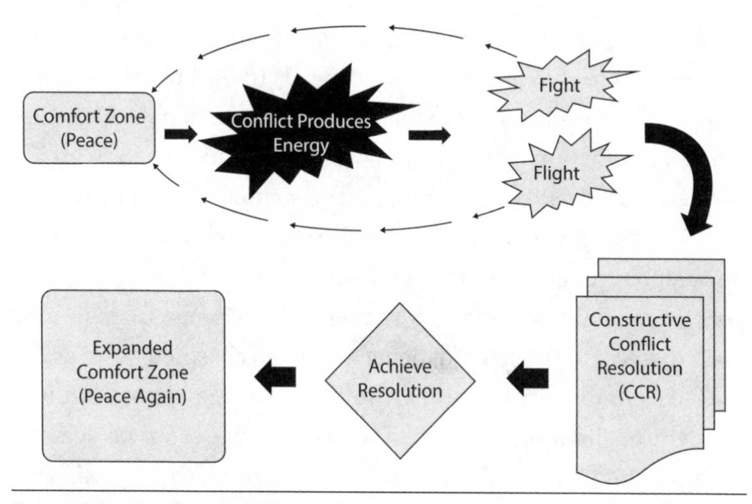

Figure 9.3. Growing through conflict

STEP 1: BLESS AND LISTEN TO BECOME AWARE

We live in a world where we jump to conclusions about other people so often we don't even realize we're doing it. Everybody is a self-appointed critic. We judge as if we know more about other people than they do, as if we know the real issue behind their problems. This practice of jumping to conclusions is illustrated every time I walk through the checkout aisle at the grocery store. Magazines live off of jumping to conclusions about people based on limited knowledge. And we feed off it. But Jesus said, "Do not judge, and you will not be judged. Do not condemn, and you will not be condemned" (Luke 6:37).

Every judgment presupposes that we are in a position of superiority over another person, that we are "god" relative to the other. It's easy for leaders to get caught in the superiority trap. Someone shares a problem in a group or with us one on one. We observe their life and their patterns. We learn their story. And feelings of superiority arise. Critical words come out. We know what their problem is and we know what they should do to change.

Playing "god" like this is exhausting. Solutions based on limited information lead to judgment, which leads to misguided direction. The job of the leader is not to play "god" for other people. No one is created to function from a position of superiority. We have no life in and of ourselves to dispense to others. Without God as our center, we are not a source of life but a vacuum that sucks life from others through our judgments. Mother Teresa once said that if you judge people, you have no time to love them. Real change is something that emerges from a sense of being loved and accepted as we are.

When conflict arises, it is easy to think we are pressing through the fight-or-flight impulse when we assess the person or persons experiencing the conflict. After all, we are not responding in emotion. This is especially easy for leaders to do because we often think our position gives us a special vantage point or insight. However, it's judgment even if we intend to be helpful. And it drives people back into their old comfort zones.

When we are tempted to jump to conclusions about others, the best thing to do is to stop, bless and listen. Our job as God's children is to bless others because we are humble enough to know that we are not fully aware of what's going on. We bless by being thankful for them, even when we don't want to be thankful. We bless by praying for them, even when we don't want to pray for them. And we bless by taking the time to listen and seek understanding of where they are coming from. In many ways, we listen people into change. We listen so that they can listen to themselves and see the reality of what God wants to do in their lives.

STEP 2: REMEMBER RIGHTLY THE WRONG DONE SO AS TO GENERATE UNDERSTANDING

Miroslav Volf's book *The End of Memory: Remembering Rightly in a Violent World* speaks to how we tend to remember the wrongs done to us. Volf challenges us to remember these things "rightly"—

that is, we must understand them truthfully and honestly. Often we fail to understand a conflict accurately because we either make the conflict less than what it is or blow it out of proportion and allow it to consume us. Either way we remember wrongly.[7] We must remember the pain rightly before we can move forward to healing, forgiveness and reconciliation.

Remembering wrongly occurs in groups all the time. When we downplay conflict, we whitewash our pain. We gravitate toward pleasing memories and avoid things that bring discomfort, especially when the discomfort goes to the core of our soul—including the parts we'd rather avoid. Instead of understanding what's going on inside of us, we put up with wrongs and excuse the actions of others. Often we do this because we think it's the Christian thing to do. We cover up memory with the call to be "nice." We try to do an end run around our memories and force themselves into some kind of resolution. Usually this results in some form of "You win, I lose" state where we stuff our feelings down while on the surface it looks like the conflict is over. But such forced resolutions are founded on the lie of remembering wrongly. We have to do the work of being honest with ourselves and others about what's going on in our souls during times of conflict. This takes time, patience, time alone with the Lord and honest processing as a group.

Groups also experience the opposite problem when they blow conflict out of proportion. Usually this happens when victims hold on to their victimization. And often the issue goes much deeper than it first appears. Suppose Jason makes a sarcastic comment about Jennifer's attire. Jennifer at first withdraws because she usually gives in to the flight impulse. But then she decides that this time she's going to be honest. In the next meeting she tells Jason how she feels and uses all kinds of blame language. A rush of relief comes over her, while Jason wonders what he did wrong. After they talk for a few more minutes, the leader realizes that Jennifer's issue goes much deeper than this one incident with Jason. The meeting has been turned upside-down and everyone wonders if they can get back to the lesson.

Something like this actually happened in a group I was part of. After the eruption we had to take a break and pray for a minute. The leader acknowledged the tension but also confessed that we would not be able to fix it in a few minutes at such an emotional moment. He then led the group in a short time of worship and the rest of the evening was spent sharing about the week and praying for one another.

During some conversations outside the meeting with Jennifer, it became clear that Jason reminded Jennifer of her father, who used to make fun of how she dressed. She had not thought about this since her father's death ten years earlier. Jennifer and the group had to remember rightly to attain an understanding of what was going on.

STEP 3: PRAY

Prayer makes a difference. In conflict, we have the opportunity to press into the way of Jesus as we pray. Bonhoeffer wrote:

> A Christian community either lives by the intercessory prayers of its members for one another or the community will be destroyed. I can no longer condemn or hate other Christians for whom I pray, no matter how much trouble they may cause me. In intercessory prayer the face that may have been strange or intolerable to me is transformed into the face of one for whom Christ died, the face of a pardoned sinner. That is a blessed discovery for the Christian who is beginning to offer intercessory prayer for others. . . . Intercessory prayer is the purifying bath into which the individual and the community must enter every day.[8]

STEP 4: DEAL WITH IT

It takes wisdom to know when it's time to bring conflict out into the open and deal honestly with the issues. Sometimes this needs to happen as quickly as possible, while other cases need to be handled more slowly. Sometimes the entire group should be part of the process, while in other cases the issue relates only to a smaller set of relationships within the group. Whatever the case, when the time comes to deal with the issues, here are some basic guidelines:

- Set a specific time and date.
- Set a time limit on the conversation so people do not become exhausted by the length of the meeting.
- Set times for future meetings to deal with issues that require further discussion.
- Define the steps that need to be taken in order to resolve the conflict. Address questions like who should talk first, how long each person should speak, and how parties will respond to interruptions and sarcasm.
- Decide if a neutral third party is needed.
- Meet at a place that is safe and neutral for everyone involved.[9]

STEP 5: LET GO

When we remember rightly, we move toward a place of letting go. If we don't let go, the conflict will define us, and it will likely recur in the future in a different form with different people, even though we withdraw back into our former comfort zone. If we don't let go, the conflict will tie us down and keep us from experiencing the new future that God wants to create through us. Pastor Brain Zahnd describes this process: "Unforgiveness has a devastating way of eliminating new possibilities. Everything remains chained to the past, and the suffered injustice becomes the single informing event in the life of the embittered soul. But the choice to forgive breaks the tyranny of injustice and the bitterness it seeks to create."[10]

When we do let go, we create space for new opportunities where the Spirit is opening doors into a new future. It's as if conflict tills the soil and, as we let go, the seed bursts forth to produce something we did not expect. To facilitate the experience of letting go, there are three things that leaders can do:

Let go of the outcome and take authority over the process. Leaders cannot force people to let go. The hoped-for outcome is that those in conflict will forgive and receive forgiveness and enlarge their comfort zone. Jennifer has to choose to forgive her father. If she doesn't she might put up with Jason for a season, but her choices will continue to impact the group. Jason also has a choice to let go of hurtful patterns, even though he does not intend them to be hurtful. While leaders cannot control the people involved in conflict, they can lay out the choices they face.

Let go of other people and take authority over your responses to them. Some people will get it. They will embrace one another and change in the midst of the conflict. Others will go through the motions, thinking they get it. Still others will need to work through long-ignored pain and rejection before they walk in the freedom God desires for them. Leaders can take authority only over their own responses. Here's a basic rule: when conflict arises, even when we are not directly involved, the first question to ask is how we need to change in the midst of the conflict.

Let go of your circumstances and take authority over the decisions you make within them. Life happens when we are making other plans. Challenges will come, and they can be seen as barriers to the group's growth or stepping stones for God's activity. If the leader sees them as barriers, he will try to control the circumstance. If he sees them as stepping stones, he will walk with authority and ask God what he is doing in the midst of these circumstances.[11]

STEP 6: AFFIRM DIFFERENCES

When my wife and I had our second child, people told us we would not be able to parent him the way we did our first. Now that we have four, I can readily say that this is true. They each are so very different, even though they share the same gene pool and are being raised in the same house. Their differences become most obvious during times of conflict. Conflict highlights how we stand out from one another and are not made to be carbon copies.

Conflict provides an opportunity for a group to realize that the other person is a gift and the gift is always unique. John Zizioulas writes, "Love is the assertion that one exists as 'other,' that is, particularly unique, *in relation to* some 'other' who affirms him or her as 'other.' In love, relation generates otherness; it does not threaten it."[12]

At this point in the process, we can easily assume that the goal is to get over the conflict and get back to the way things were. The new normal is supposed to be a continuation of the old normal. But when we do this we end up with a predetermined uniformity.

Many mistake uniformity for unity. When we seek uniformity we either force people into our mold or we drive them away. I saw an extreme case of uniformity when a pastor told me that he had mentored his team to such a degree that if you asked any of them a question, they would answer it the same way he would. In situations like these, the goal is unity, but it becomes false agreement where no one has a perspective, a point of view or a personal identity. Dissenting voices are a problem; those who present different perspectives are in rebellion against leadership. The way to deal with conflict is to squelch it as quickly as possible and get on with the vision.

In predetermined uniformity, the people with the power set the agenda and the voices of the marginalized remain marginalized. The perspective of the outsider does not get heard, which means that people who don't fit the pattern are left to themselves to figure things out. When I attended my first small groups conference, the event concluded with a panel session. Someone asked about how to lead an icebreaker when people did not want open up. Four white men gave very logical answers, providing direct approaches to get people to share more openly. Everything they said made sense—if you were a man of power. But there were two women in my own group who would have been repelled by these approaches.

In that group we had to process new ways to lead icebreakers, which meant that those who did not like how the leaders did it had to step up and offer different solutions. New doors that open through conflict lead to a mosaic of differences. This is not a time for the leader to set the agenda and move on with the next step. It is a time for discovery of what has been revealed—both the good and the bad—through the conflict.

STEP 7: ENTER THE NEW COMFORT ZONE

Earlier I mentioned a conversation with a group leader where I learned that two of his group members had almost had a fistfight after Sunday morning worship. To everyone's surprise—including my own—this was exactly what this group needed. It was a large group with a few non-Christians participating in its life. Because the group worked through the issues, it moved beyond its religious safe-talk. One of the guys in the near-fistfight confessed that he did not even want to be in the group; he was just doing it for his wife. Walls came down all over the place. New Christians and baptisms resulted. And that one group became three groups. The guy who did not want to be in the group became a leader of one of the new groups.

This was a dramatic new comfort zone. Most of the time, the drama that comes with conflict is not so noteworthy. But it creates a new comfort zone nonetheless. Conflict changes who you are as it makes room in your soul: room for others, room for God and room for a new freedom to be yourself.

Point the Way to the Cross

The Eighth Practice

I wish the way of Jesus looked and felt like a steady progressive journey to higher and higher points in our walk with God. If I were to chart my hopes and dreams for my leadership and its impact on the world, it would look something like this (see fig. 10.1).

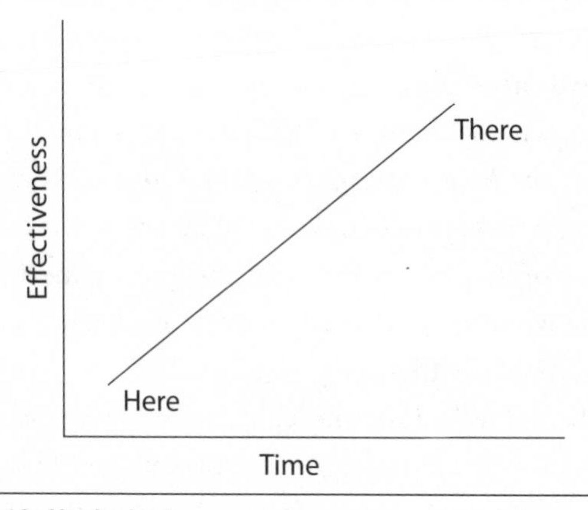

Figure 10.1. The ideal leadership journey

The reality, though, is quite different. I've never found that leading people follows such a predictable path. It always looks more like an adventure of agony and ecstasy. At the beginning of a group, the growth experience might feel like a straight, rising line, but then the ups and downs of reality set in. It might be graphed this way (see fig. 10.2).

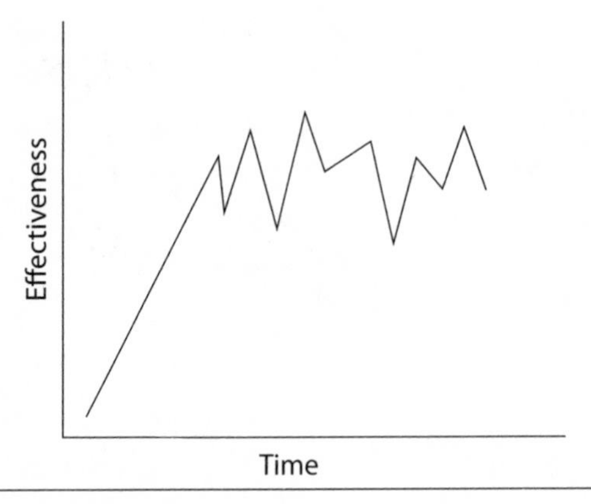

Figure 10.2. Group growth experience

In *The Fellowship of the Ring,* the first book of *The Lord of the Rings* trilogy, we are introduced to a group of nine individuals who volunteer for a specific task. They have a concrete, intentional mission—to destroy an evil, powerful ring—and they set out toward the one place where the ring can be destroyed. But at the end of *The Fellowship of the Ring,* the group is attacked and its members are split up. One person is killed, two hobbits are captured, two other hobbits head off to destroy the ring, and three expert fighters are left standing wondering what to do next. The plan is not working. In fact, one might say that the plan has failed.

This is where *The Two Towers* begins—and where the story twists. Logic, strategic planning and good leadership would say the three strongest fighters should remain focused on the primary cause, that of destroying the ring. Instead they chase after the two captured hobbits. Now if you know the story, you know that these two hobbits are not good fighters. They're more than a bit irresponsible, and they're tagging along with no understanding of what they got themselves into when they volunteered for the mission. So here we have three heroes going in the opposite direction from their original purpose and chasing after two hobbits who are not equipped to contribute much to that purpose.

If this is not a picture of group leadership, then I don't know what is. You and the group set out with the best of intentions. You pray. You read books on the subject. The group wrestles with what this community means for their lives. You work at it. You even see progress along the way. You discover new insights into how you relate to one another and to the world.

Then things happen. Life happens. Sometimes it's negative stuff that we might attribute to an attack from Satan. Sometimes it's just the normal stuff of life. We find our path less than straight. Instead of going in the direction we'd planned, we put our energy into something else entirely. Instead of progressing toward our goal, we end up taking two steps back.

Failure, death, the cross. We expect God to work through our leadership successes, but the place of death and struggle is actually where God's work of deep change takes place, the kind that realigns our being to our intentions. We set out thinking we can advance the way of Jesus, a vision that God has given us. But God takes us all the way down into death in order to reorient our being around the way of Jesus.

As leaders we have to learn to give people the space for God to do this work. This means that our job is to go to the cross and make space for others to go to the cross.

DEEP CHANGE

Following God never leads us along a straight path. The way of relating to God and others in love is always full of mystery. We assume we know how each step should go, leading us ever closer to what we think is our calling and destiny. The three warriors in *The Lord of the Rings*, Aragorn, Legolas and Gimli, thought they were going forth on a direct course to destroy a ring. But they found themselves running across fields and up and down mountains seeking to save two small hobbits who to that point had done nothing but bungle things up.

When you get to the end of the story, you see how what looked like a wasteful diversion for the warriors was actually the path that would lead them to climax of the story. Without the diversion, without the mystery, without the unexpected twist that comes through failure, there is no story at all.

When people venture out on the journey, they begin with great intentions. A group attains a clear vision through conversation, reading and asking the right questions. This kind of change is visible and even measurable. It's like the top of an iceberg. We can see it when people set their intentions and minds through commitment to the way of Jesus. We can even see it when people carry out their intentions through concrete means—that is, through tangible structures and processes.[1] We need clear vision, decisions of intent and concrete means for carrying out the vision. But there is more.

Beneath the water line is the need to change how we relate to others. In some ways we have control over this and we can implement the vision-intention-means approach to relational change. But in many ways, it is a realm beyond our full control. We try to relate well. We try to invest in our neighbors and our networks. We adopt the means for dealing with conflict as outlined by all the best resources. Sometimes it works; other times it just falls flat. But we are changed in the process because we are relating to others in a different way. The change never looks like what we expect, but we are different nonetheless.

But there is a deeper level to the iceberg (see fig. 10.3).[2]

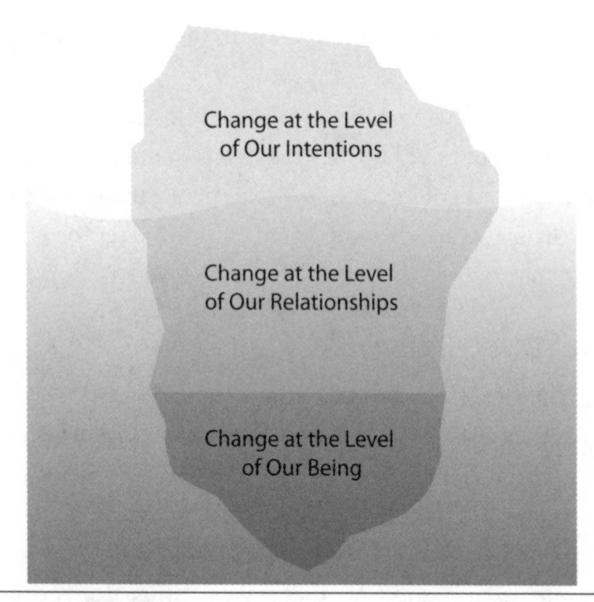

Figure 10.3. Three levels of change

Here we experience what can only be described as death. Jesus said, "Unless a kernel of wheat falls to the ground and dies, it remains only a single seed. But if it dies, it produces many seeds" (John 12:24). In order for the seeds within us to activate and grow into community and mission, we must die. This means we must make space for people to take up their cross daily and follow Jesus (Luke 9:23).

By this I do not mean engaging in some kind of ongoing, self-deprecating guilt that highlights how we are unworthy, scum-filled sinners. Nor is this a reference to the need to see our guilt as a part of a conversion experience. This is about the reality that we all face: that resurrection life comes on the other side of the cross. Victory is found on the other side of coming to the end of ourselves. Flourishing is a gift we realize when we work through failure. Those who embrace this reality and allow others to fail will create space for people to go to the cross and receive the resurrection.

Those who don't end up like Judas Iscariot, stuck in the fact that things did not work out like they wanted them to. They embrace a death that keeps them in death. We experience this when we avoid the cross, when we avoid the reality of failure and try to control our way to victory.

REFUSE TO FIX

When people face struggles in life, whether personally or relationally, our natural tendency as leaders is to help them get over the struggle so they can get back to normal. We don't want them to have to endure the pain that comes with struggle. We don't want them to fail. As a result, we try to fix the situation. We offer advice or come up with a solution that turns things around quickly, thinking that we're being there for the person who's struggling.

But our fixing gets in the way of what the other person truly needs. The other person needs to go all the way to the cross with the situation. She doesn't need someone who will save her from the struggle, thereby interrupting the deep change that the Spirit of God wants to bring about. She needs people who will walk with her and point her along the path that will connect her to Christ in the midst of the struggle. Bonhoeffer put it this way:

> Spiritual love will prove successful insofar as it commends Christ to the other in all that is says and does. It will not seek to agitate another by exerting all to personal, direct influence or by crudely interfering in one's life. It will not take pleasure in pious, emotional fervor and excitement. Rather, it will encounter the other with the clear word of God and be prepared to leave the other alone with this word for a long time. It will be willing to release others again so that Christ may deal with

> them. It will respect the other as the boundary that Christ establishes between us; and it will find full community with the other in the Christ who alone binds us together. This spiritual love will thus speak to Christ about the other Christian more than to the other Christian about Christ. It knows that the most direct way to others is always through prayer to Christ and that love of the other is completely tied to the truth found in Christ.[3]

The fix-it options we adopt assume that we need to relate to the other person directly. When I try to fix another person, I'm trying to attach that person to myself and projecting my own experience or perspective onto him or her. Our perspective causes us to read others' pain and struggle through our own point of view. But of course this never gets us anywhere close to what's really going on. This way of relating to others is so common that we don't even recognize we are doing it. And our perspective ultimately causes us to judge the other person, even when we think we're being compassionate. We are trying to remove the speck in the other's eye when we have a plank in our own. In other words, we jump to conclusions about the other person's needs because we assume we have enough information to come to an accurate solution.

Only God has enough information to come to an accurate assessment. And the shocker is that his reaction to this information was to become incarnate and go to the cross. Instead of castigating or condemning those who struggle, he died for their sake (Romans 5:8). Instead of fixing people in the midst of their pain, he died and invited others to follow him on that way.

The reason we cannot fix people through direct love is because we do not naturally think about loving the other at any cost to ourselves, especially when the one we are called to love is struggling. When we try to fix the situation, we are often doing so because it makes it easier for us or for the group to move on. The only way to love another person is indirectly. We can love only through Jesus because he is the only one who sees the other properly and the only one who responds by going to the cross for the other.

The most practical way to live this out is to pray for the other. Instead of jumping to conclusions, instead of trying to fix the situation, instead of acting like nothing has happened, instead of complaining or gossiping, instead of _________ (fill in the blank with your natural reaction when people are struggling), live in the ambiguity of prayer. See the other as walking a journey carrying a huge backstory about which you know very little. See the other as walking in the midst of struggles that you have never walked. See the other as moving forward on a path with Jesus walking alongside, directing the person toward a hopeful future you cannot see.

When we do this, we enter into the work of Jesus as he leads the person to the cross. This is where the deep change to our being occurs. We walk with the person through the struggle. We don't judge. We don't try to get the person out of the struggle. We refuse to provide easy solutions. We point out the way to the cross and give the person the space to go all the way.

TO THE CROSS

The only way I know how to explain what I'm talking about when referring to deep change is to offer an experience. About three years ago I was working with a church in Washington. I had sat in a recording studio for a day and a half, filming twenty-four segments of teaching. I was emotionally spent and exhausted, but I still had two days of work to do with this church. On top of this, I was in the midst of a time of great failure. My wife and I had made some major life changes that were not working out. My business was not getting off the ground. More than anything I was coming to terms with the reality that I was not the center of the universe.

I had begun to see how much of my spirituality had been shaped by messages like "How I can be happy?" "How I can be saved?" "How I can be a great spiritual leader?" or "How I can make a difference for God?"

At the end of this recording session, I told the project director I needed to go for a walk. I headed to the prayer garden located on the church campus, where I noticed a labyrinth. A prayer labyrinth is an intricately designed path intended to facilitate prayer and meditation as you walk through the maze. At the center of this particular labyrinth was a cross (see fig. 10.4).

Figure 10.4. Prayer labyrinth

While I had read a lot about praying through a labyrinth, I had never done so myself. Others had told me how issues and emotions arise within you unexpectedly when you pray this way, but I had no logical framework for understanding what they meant. I had walked and prayed many times. What was the difference? I ventured through the garden toward the opening.

As I neared the entrance, which at first I could not locate, I found myself not wanting to step inside. I wanted to keep walking and get back to work. It's not that I was afraid of meeting with God or that I was full of pride and self-sufficiency. I'd reached the point where I had nothing left and I was so tired there was no energy for pride. What I did have, I realized at that point, was a core fear. I was afraid that meeting with God would be less than what I expected—that he might not even be there to meet with me.

Here's the truth: I find it easier to try to follow God without depending on his presence. It's simpler to do community and mission without a trip to the cross. After all, we know what God wants us to do. We've been taught to evangelize, to feed the poor, to love our neighbors. Why do we need that daily journey to the cross? And so we resist. I've heard preachers confront this resistance all my life, explaining that we're selfish, self-sufficient and self-diluted. And while these characteristics are a part of why we resist going to the cross, I've found that they're only a facade masking much greater fears within.

Mine was a fear that God might not be there to meet with me. My Bible teaching about how God would never leave me did not matter at that moment within the core of my being. This was not about logic. This was about my deep experience of God. What I assumed was pride was actually a deep, illogical dread. I learned something new about myself and what keeps me from the Jesus way.

WALKING TO THE CROSS

I finally entered the labyrinth. As I walked, I realized something major was going on deep inside me. All my logical walls were trying to go up: Why would walking through a labyrinth help me open my heart to God? But I pushed aside logic and walked. With every turn through the maze, more things rose within me. Within ten steps I began pouring out my heart to God. I recounted pains and disappointments, frustrations and even bitterness. I yelled. I screamed. I cried. I saw my failure—both things I had done and the things done to me—flashing before my eyes. As I walked toward the center, which was marked by a cross, all this stuff came up that I did not even realize was weighing me down—things I needed to release at the cross.

This experience reminds me of Jesus' words about discipleship in Luke 9:23-24: "Whoever wants to be my disciple must deny themselves and take up their cross daily and follow me. For whoever wants to save their life will lose it, but whoever loses their life for me will save it." Admittedly, I've heard this passage quoted hundreds of times. I've even preached on it. But it came to life in me. The words "deny self" gained new meaning. This was not about me losing my identity or denying that I had something to offer God and the world. This was not some platonic version of "all of God and none of me."

This was about pulling back the false me, that which covers up who God made me to be. It was the denial of things like performing for others' approval, fighting to attain security in this life, putting hope in self-reliance and fearing failure. As I walked and poured out my heart to God, I recounted the journey of the last year—how God had brought about incredible inside-out transformation, raising deep questions of the soul that strip bare all false pretenses, even good false pretenses.

I was seeing how the failures were pulling away the things that covered up the real me. I was seeing how I had hidden myself from being loved and loving others. I was seeing how I was trying to lead out of performance and trying to fulfill others' expectations for me. I was tired of trying to make community and mission in the way of Jesus happen. And I saw how little I was able to do to make it happen.

AT THE CROSS

Jesus said that those who would be his disciples—those who would be shaped by his life—would develop a way of cross-carrying. When I was deep inside the labyrinth, I finally came to the cross at the center. I stopped and just gazed at the cross, which was formed by rocks lying on the ground. Here is where a great exchange occurred in my encounter with God. All the pain, disappointment and failure that I was experiencing and that had arisen within my soul as I prayed through the first half of the labyrinth fell off me. It was like I had a new freedom to let go of the crushing burden that had been weighing me down.

In exchange, I was given more than "new life" or "abundant life," which is often the focus of conversations about the exchange that occurs at the cross. I was given a cross of my own to bear, one of sharing in the life of Jesus for the sake of the world. My imagination about my calling took on another level of meaning as I stood at the cross. I was captured by a new way of being. I'm not called to make the church bigger and better—although that might be a legitimate result. I'm not called to make my ministry bigger and better. I'm called to take up my cross, the specific one Jesus has given to me so I can contribute to a "for the sake of the world" kind of life.

Of course, most of us state that we follow Jesus and minister for the sake of the world. But I've had too many conversations with other ministers where our words gave away our true motivations. We were ministering for things like

- the sake of growing "my" church
- the sake of advancing my ministry
- the sake of people's praise
- the sake of "getting our theology right"

- the sake of being "missional"
- the sake of ________________

When we take that approach, we carry burdens that are not ours. We are so focused on ourselves and what we produce that we miss what God wants: to reform our hearts so we can freely love the world. When we release these burdens at the cross, we receive in exchange a freedom to love for the sake of God's redemption of the world.

IN THE TOMB

After walking away from the cross at the center of the labyrinth, I began to reflect on the death I had experienced. In some ways, this was a tomblike experience, one that comes after death but before resurrection. It was a time of silence, of waiting, of isolation. You see, there is a lot of noise at the foot of the cross and even more on the journey toward the cross. But once we have released that which weighs us down at the cross, the next experience is not usually one of joyous victory and exaltation. I've found that after I die to something and give it over to Jesus, what follows is a haunting loneliness of waiting for the resurrection.

I'd rather go immediately to the resurrection part. Victory is the stuff that we preach. However, the time of haunting loneliness that follows death forms us for resurrection life. When we try to jump straight to victory, it's too easy to relapse into old patterns, into old stuff we laid down at the cross.

For instance, let's say that in meeting Jesus at the cross, you realize that you need to die to the approval of others. To walk in resurrection victory would mean that you cease being concerned about what people think about you. However, if your life has been shaped by decades of living for the approval of others, then your thought patterns, your actions and your feelings have been formed by this search for approval. You may very well have given it over to

Jesus, but the next step is to learn how to develop new ways of thinking, acting and feeling that do not depend on others' approval. This "tomb" experience can feel very lonely. Everything you have depended on in the past is not there to lean on. And the new patterns are undeveloped.

In the tomb, we lose control over how the resurrection will occur. We know that we are dead to the past, but we have not yet fully entered into new freedom. In this no man's land we experience formation by and of the Spirit. Notice the emphasis. This is the time of transformation by and of the Spirit, the mysterious inner working that is done in us, not that we make happen. This is not a control experience where I activate God in my life to enter into resurrection victory. My part is simply to make room for the Spirit to develop in me new capacities to walk out of the tomb and into the victory of the resurrection.

This often happens as we develop new habits. This is one of the ways that we participate in the re-formation of the Spirit. Research has demonstrated that it usually takes about sixty-six days to develop a new habit or routine. It takes lots of repetition (and failure) to get new practices into our gut to the point that they become second nature.[4]

OUT FROM THE TOMB

As I was praying through the last few steps of the labyrinth, I found that I did not want it to end. I slowed my pace. I felt myself wanting to sit down and stay there for a bit. I had responsibilities that needed addressing. Staying put was not an option. Even still, I wanted to escape, to avoid those responsibilities. I wanted to enter into some kind of romantic experience with Jesus and let him continue his work of inner formation in my life.

I realized that it is easier to remain in the tomb with Jesus than to walk with him in the real world. It's easier to escape into our private encounters with Jesus than to live resurrection at work, with our families, with our neighbors or during our mundane, everyday responsibilities. I think this is one reason we so easily separate the sacred from the secular. A labyrinth experience is a sacred thing. Worship on Sunday is a sacred experience. Small groups are God things where we do God stuff. But when we walk out, we enter the world of the secular. It's not always clear how the sacred weaves into all of life.

I wanted to hold on to my encounter with God, but if I had done that I would have left my experience of Jesus in the tomb until I could return. A labyrinth has an exit. We enter the prayer labyrinth (or whatever way you might pray) to encounter God, to let go of baggage, to allow the Spirit to transform us and prepare us, but ultimately the labyrinth opens up into the world. Jesus is moving by the Spirit in the world all around us. We pray to have our senses trained so that we can become fully aware of what Jesus is doing and join in.

At the exit of the labyrinth, I realized that it's a lot easier to remain stuck in our questions, in our hangups, in our unknowing, in our inabilities, in our self-doubt—all the stuff we have to deal with in the loneliness of the tomb—than it is to take a risk and walk the journey with Jesus on his mission. We fall in love with the darkness of the tomb and wait for some kind of enlightenment experience that will miraculously pick us up and lead us into the resurrection life. Jesus was raised from the dead by the power of the Spirit, but once the rock was rolled back, he had to put one foot in front of the other. The same is true for us. The rock is rolled back. Resurrection life has been given to us as a gift. Will we walk out and join Jesus in what he is doing in our world?

DANCING TO THE CROSS

As I have reflected on my labyrinth experience, I have come to see that I was not walking through it, although that's what I was doing physically. I was figuratively dancing back and forth through the maze, learning new steps that moved me toward the cross. And then I paused at the cross, as if the music had stopped playing. When the music began again, I danced away from the cross, learning new steps that would prepare me to dance afresh outside the tomb.

Theologians often refer to the life of God as *perichoresis,* which is a word that means something like a commingled dance of unity between the Father, Son and Spirit. This dance describes the love shared between the members of the Trinity, which defines who God is from eternity. As I prayed through the labyrinth, I was learning the dance steps of the Trinity that day.

This was the way of Jesus as he danced with the Father and the Spirit as recorded in the Gospels. After the baptism in the Jordan River, the Father spoke: "You are my Son, whom I love; with you I am well pleased" (Mark 1:11), and the Spirit descended on him like a dove. Jesus walked in communion with the Father through the power of the Spirit. He did only what he saw the Father doing already (John 5:19). He spent excessive time with the Father (Mark 1:35). The way of Jesus is the way of dancing communion.

While Jesus walked in perfect communion with God, our journey is different. As we enter the way of Jesus we enter a dance school where the Spirit teaches us the triune dance steps. At first they are superficial and may even be foreign to us—the upper level of the iceberg. Then as we practice these steps with others they shape us and start to become second nature, especially when we are together—illustrated by the middle level of the iceberg. But the dance of the Spirit seeks to form us down in the core of our being, illustrated by the bottom layer of the iceberg.

We learn these steps together as we step out with others who are committed to the way of Jesus. Most of this book has been focused on how we dance together. At the same time, we dance best together when we also dance in solitude. Bonhoeffer gave us a twofold warning about this: "Whoever cannot be alone should beware of community. . . . Alone you had to take up your cross, struggle, and pray and alone you will die and give an account to God." Then he wrote, "Whoever cannot stand being in community should beware of being alone. . . . You carry your cross, you struggle and you pray in the community of faith, the community of those who are called."[5]

Just as I had to enter the labyrinth alone, so must each one of us. Part of the job of leading others in the way of Jesus is to point individuals to the cross. There are times when the only way to step further along the way of Jesus is to enter the space of solitude. Each has to sit at the cross with the private pain and struggle that ultimately only Jesus can see.

When leading people, we need to point to the labyrinth. We cannot force the victory of resurrection life. We cannot force people to hear the rhythms of the Jesus way (as pointed out in the first practice). We cannot stir up enough emotion to make the presence of Jesus happen (the second practice). We cannot recruit enough leaders to be a part of the team (the third practice). We could say this about all of the practices outlined in this book. Ultimately, our call is to enter into the dance with God and make space for others to join. Too often leaders assume that it is their job to make things happen, and by doing so they actually get in the way of the work of the Spirit. Every individual contributes to the group's ability to dance. But at the same time, the group must give each individual the space to dance their way to the cross and thereby give them the room needed to die and rise again.

Leaders do this as they embrace the mystery of prayer. We pray as a group. We pray as leadership teams. We pray as individuals. We go on prayer walks. We lead meetings that focus the entire night on prayer.

We pray for each other. We pray for ourselves. We pray and we pray because we know that this is not about what we can make happen. The way of Jesus is a way of community and mission, but it's God's dance of community and God's dance of mission that matters.

So we pray. We pray so that we can enter into and receive that which we cannot make happen.

Part of this prayer requires us to learn practical ways that will shape our way of praying. This is technical in nature. Using *lectio divina* can help you along this path as it will teach you to pray the Scriptures (as mentioned in Practice Six). Or simply devoting daily time to pray through the Lord's Prayer line by line is helpful. However, this is more than technique. This is about relationship. It's about learning to talk, walk and respond to God.

DANCING WELL

The dance of the Trinity is about learning how to respond to the steps of the way of God. He is leading this dance, not us. One way to learn the dance steps is illustrated by the Ignatian Examen. This was a spiritual discipline developed by Saint Ignatius to help people see how God has been at work in their lives, or in people around them, in unexpected ways. This is a simple process of slowing down and reflecting on a specific time period (maybe a day or a week) and asking a few questions that helps you see how God has been at work. By allowing thoughts to arise in your mind, as opposed to working to formulate an answer, it makes room in your spirit to listen to the Holy Spirit. Some basic listening questions might include:

- In what ways and places have you seen God challenge you (or the group) beyond the status quo?
- When has God's presence become real to you (or to the group) in unexpected times?
- How has God connected you with others in ways you did not predict?
- How has God cared for another through you?

- When have you had to change as you related to others?
- When have you seen opportunities to hang out with others and share life?
- Where have there been struggles or conflicts within you or in relationships?
- What has energized you or the group?
- What circumstances have depleted your energy?

As we listen to what God is doing, we are better able to join the dance and point others to the cross. We are able to make room for people to come to the end of themselves and die, which thereby makes room for resurrection life. We cannot make resurrection life. We can change our intentions to line up with that vision. We can align our lives with others who are committed to the same thing. But we must realize that God is at work to draw us into community and make room for us to participate in his mission to redeem the world. This is the way of Jesus. This is God's dance, and most likely the dance steps God is taking will surprise you.

The job of the leader is to create an environment where people dance their way to the cross. This kind of leadership is not about controlling people so that they do a specified list of tasks that have proven to produce the fruit of life together. Nor is this kind of leadership an option that we can do part of the time while the rest of the time we depend on other ways of leading.

In order for group members to journey to the cross and out from the tomb, we have to lead in such a way that the Spirit resides in and among us in our groups, even when we don't fully see or understand what the Spirit is doing. This trust is most needed when group members encounter their own form of failure, when Sarah and Jim hit a rough patch in their marriage, when Tom loses his job and cannot find a new one, when Terri gets sick and cannot take care of the kids, when Traci's kids walk away from the church. It's tempting to try to fix things, but the Spirit is in the midst of the mess, taking us all the way to the cross. This journey to the cross could be the very thing that launches the group into a serendipitous experience that transforms the group and touches others outside it. It could be the key that opens the door to that which we long to experience the most.

Dancing with the triune God on the path to the cross is the way of Jesus. It is the mystery of the life of God and the paradoxical way that God works to restore all things in this world. It does not make sense, but it's true.

conclusion

Living the Story of the Jesus Way

The way of Jesus is a story. The Bible does not give us a meticulous plan for how to walk in the Jesus way. We have a story, one that begins with creation and moves forward with rebellion, the life of Israel with YHWH. Then we have the story of Jesus, the early church and the complete restoration of all things at the end of time.

Our groups are a part of this grand, all-encompassing story. Over the years I've observed that groups typically tell one of four stories. They are not about the vision the leaders have cast or the stated purpose of the group. Neither are they about what we call our groups, whether that's house churches, cell groups, missional communities, life groups or community groups. The name of the group doesn't make the story. And the stories we tell have little to do with what we are studying in our group meetings. Although having good curriculum is helpful, the stories we tell are about how we live out what we are studying, not the study itself.

Nor is the story about the great talents and gifts of the leader. This is not a story about any one person. It's a story about God and God's redemption of all things. Our groups tell stories that make or break the life of a group. Here they are.

The first story is called *personal improvement.* This is the small group experience where individuals participate because it is personally beneficial. The people involved are either drawn to a topic or to a group of people like themselves, and participation is high until it becomes inconvenient. Nothing in group members' personal life is required to change to participate. The key distinctive of this story is that people attend as long as it benefits them.

Lifestyle adjustment identifies the second story. People view such groups as beneficial, and therefore group members are willing to adjust their life schedules to prioritize attendance at a weekly or biweekly meeting. Usually people make longer-term commitments to attend such groups because they're good for one's spiritual journey. But the group is not great. It's a good-meeting group that requires some adjustment in schedules, but most often there's little commitment to living out community and mission beyond the group meetings. The key distinctive is that people make schedule adjustments to prioritize meeting regularly.

The third story is called *relational re-vision.* In this narrative, groups have a sense of urgency to operate according to a distinct set of practices that will form them into a community that stands out in our world. They recognize that loving one another does not come naturally in an individualistic, fast-paced culture that dominates modern life. They know that they have to learn a new way of living, that it will take practice and that it will take time. The key distinctive here is that the small group is committed to learning how to live in community with one another in a way that stands in contrast to typical patterns of life.

Missional re-creation describes the final story. As a group begins to practice these distinctive patterns and the way of Jesus becomes part of its being, the group will follow the Spirit on creative paths of life together as members engage the community. They will engage the neighborhood, determine needs, meet those needs and, as a result, change as a group. Some groups might develop into house churches of fifty. Others might meet in groups of five at a coffee shop. One person might meet with a group of shift workers at a bar he frequents after getting off work early in the morning. Others will adopt a home for mentally challenged individuals. And still others will come around a family that lives in a mindset of poverty and walk with them into a new way of being. The specific form is not the point. The key distinctive is that the group takes on unexpected manifestations that have an organic impact on the world around the group.

Most groups settle for one of the first two stories. Most hope for the latter two. It's tempting to judge the first two and say that they are off the way of Jesus and elevate the latter two to special Jesus way status. And while in some ways this is true, we cannot make this conclusion. All are on the way of Jesus because the Spirit of God is drawing us from where we are further down the way. We don't get to take the next step on the way from where we wish we were. Jesus works with us where we are.

Maybe your group falls into story one or two. No condemnation is called for. Only a challenge. Don't settle for it. And if you find yourself in story three or four, keep going. Don't stop now.

The eight leadership practices outlined in this book are designed to help leaders enter into the way of Jesus that is already at work in the world by the power of the Spirit. This is not about you working harder to try and make the third and fourth stories happen in your group. This is about learning to step into what God is doing in our world, being drawn up into the active life of the Spirit and moving beyond what you can produce. This is about entering into that which only God can do. With the apostle Paul, we recognize that this is a work of the triune God in our lives, as he prayed:

For this reason I kneel before the Father, from whom every family in heaven and on earth derives its name. I pray that out of his glorious riches he may strengthen you with power through his Spirit in your inner being, so that Christ may dwell in your hearts through faith. And I pray that you, being rooted and established in love, may have power, together with all the Lord's holy people, to grasp how wide and long and high and deep is the love of Christ, and to know this love that surpasses knowledge—that you may be filled to the measure of all the fullness of God.

Now to him who is able to do immeasurably more than all we ask or imagine, according to his power that is at work within us, to him be glory in the church and in Christ Jesus throughout all generations, for ever and ever! Amen. (Ephesians 3:14-21)

Acknowledgments

This book began with a short article I wrote in 2000 for *Cell Group Journal*. Thereafter, I got busy with other responsibilities and did not remember what I had written until some point in 2010. Thank you, Randall Neighbour, for the opportunity to get started down this path all those years ago. The ideas of this book were birthed out of the input of so many that it's hard to list all of them. The seeds go back to some sermons given by Alan Roxburgh and a class led by Alan Torrance. At some point along the way I began developing these ideas into training sessions that I shared at various churches. If you participated in those training events, thank you for your interaction and the feedback.

I would also like to express my gratitude to my editors David Zimmerman and Cindy Bunch for their patience and direction in this process of getting this book out. To my friend Mike Friessen, thank you for listening to me rant about ideas I could not articulate. And to my wife, Shawna, once again I acknowledge that I am more than honored to share the way of Jesus with you, particularly in the ways that you have modeled so much of this book to me. The opportunity to share this journey with you remains the greatest of joys.

Notes

CHAPTER 1: THE SEARCH FOR GREAT GROUP LEADERSHIP

[1]Joel Comiskey, *Home Cell Group Explosion* (Houston: Touch Publications, 1998), p. 26. Jim Egli and Dwight Marable, *Small Groups, Big Impact* (St. Charles, IL: ChurchSmart Resources, 2011), p. 16.

CHAPTER 2: LEADING IN THE WAY OF JESUS

[1]See Charles Duhigg, *The Power of Habit* (New York: Random House, 2012).

[2]Joel Comiskey, *Home Cell Group Explosion* (Houston: Touch Publications, 1998), p. 34.

[3]Lynn Anderson, *They Smell Like Sheep* (West Monroe, LA: Howard, 1997).

[4]The concept of adaptive leadership is explained in Ronald Heifetz, Alexander Grashow and Marty Linsky, *The Practice of Adaptive Leadership* (Boston: Harvard Business Press, 2009).

[5]Technical challenges call for technical leadership, while adaptive challenges call for adaptive leadership. Leadership expert Ronald Heifetz writes, "Problems are *technical* in the sense that we know already how to respond to them. . . . These problems are technical because the necessary knowledge about them already has been digested and put in the form of a legitimized set of known organizational procedures guiding what to do and role authorizations guiding who should do it." *Leadership Without Easy Answers* (Cambridge, MA: Belknap, 1994), pp. 71-72. The technical practices of group leadership tend to be the focus of most small group leader training modules, books and websites.

[6]Ibid., p. 73.

[7]Tim Morey, *Embodying Our Faith* (Downers Grove, IL: InterVarsity Press, 2009), p. 111.

[8]The classic definition of a practice has been set by the eminent ethicist Alasdair MacIntyre in his magisterial book *After Virtue*: "By a 'practice' I am going to mean any coherent and complex form of socially established cooperative human activity through which goods internal to that form of activity are realized in the course of trying to achieve those standards of excellence which are appropriate to and partially definitive of, that form of activity, with the result that human powers to achieve excellence, and human conceptions of the ends of goods involved, are systematically extended." (South Bend, IN: University of Notre Dame Press, 1984), p. 187.

[9]Craig Dykstra and Dorothy C. Bass, "Times of Yearning, Practices of Faith" in *Practicing our Faith* (San Francisco: Jossey-Bass, 1997), p. 5.

[10]Craig Dykstra, *Growing in the Life of Faith* (Louisville, KY: Westminster John Knox, 2005), p. 66.

[11]Ibid., p. 56.

[12]"Christian practices are patterns of cooperative human activity in and through which life together takes shape over time in response to and in God as known in Jesus Christ." Dorothy C. Bass, "Introduction" in *Practicing Theology,* ed. Miroslav Volf and Dorothy C. Bass (Grand Rapids: Eerdmans, 2002), p. 3.

"Virtues are derived from repeated practices that a community continually performs because it regards them as central to its identity." Samuel Wells, *Improvisation: The Drama of Christian Ethics* (Grand Rapids: Brazos, 2004), p. 24. Practices form "believers who for Jesus' sake do ordinary social things differently." John Howard Yoder, *Body Politics* (Scottdale, PA: Herald, 2001), p. 75. "Practices are communal habits, engaged intentionally both to form the community in ways appropriate to that community's mission and to witness to that mission." Kristopher Norris, *Pilgrim Practices* (Eugene, OR: Cascade, 2012), p. 10. A pilgrim "adopts a new place and new identity by learning a new language, rhythms and practices." A person embarks upon a pilgrimage "not to escape life, but to embrace it more deeply, to be transformed wholly as a person with new ways of being in community and new hopes for the world." Diana Butler Bass, *Christianity for the Rest of Us* (San Francisco: HarperCollins, 2006), p. 216. "Practices of the Christian faith . . . are not . . . activities we do to make something happen in our lives. Nor are they duties we undertake to be obedient to God. Rather they are patterns of communal action that create openings in our lives where the grace, mercy, and presence of God may be made known to us." Dykstra, *Growing in the Life*, p. 66.

[13]Paul Froese and Christopher Bader, *America's Four Gods* (New York: Oxford University Press, 2010).

[14]John R. Franke, *The Character of Theology* (Grand Rapids: Baker Academic, 2005), p. 67.

[15]Gregory A. Boyd makes this statement in various ways in his book *Repenting of Religion* (Grand Rapids: Baker Books, 2004).

[16]In reflecting on these words, N. T. Wright states, "Bearing, believing, hoping, enduring, never failing—all these speak of moments, hours, days, and perhaps years when there will be things to bear, things to believe against apparent evidence, things to hope for which are not seen at present, things to endure, things which threaten to make love fail." *After You Believe* (New York: HarperOne, 2010), p. 182.

CHAPTER 3: HEAR THE RHYTHMS OF THE JESUS WAY: THE FIRST PRACTICE

[1]"If, then, someone were to speak to Jesus' contemporaries of YHWH's becoming king, we may safely assume that they would have in mind, in some form or other, this two-sided story concerning the double reality of exile. Israel would 'really' return from exile; YHWH would finally return to Zion. But if these were to happen there would have to be a third element as well: evil, usually in the form of Israel's enemies, must be defeated." N. T. Wright, *Jesus and the Victory of God* (Minneapolis: Fortress, 1997), p. 206.

[2]John Howard Yoder, *The Original Revolution* (Scottdale, PA: Herald, 2003), pp. 13-33.

[3]Ibid., p. 28.

[4]Ibid., p. 31.

[5]M. Scott Boren, *Missional Small Groups* (Grand Rapids: Baker Books, 2010).

[6]Henri J. M. Nouwen, *Reaching Out* (New York: Doubleday, 1975), p. 19.

[7]Ibid., p. 33.

[8]Seraphim Sigrist, *A Life Together* (Brewster, MA: Paraclete, 2011), p. 52.

[9]Ibid., pp. 49-50.

[10]Dietrich Bonhoeffer, *Life Together,* trans. Daniel Bloesch and James Burtness (Minneapolis: Fortress, 1996), p. 27.

[11]Ibid., p. 28.

[12]Jean Vanier, *Community and Growth* (New York: Paulist, 1989), p. 23.

[13]Elton Trueblood, *Alternative to Futility* (New York: Harper and Brothers, 1948), p. 74.

[14]My book *Missional Small Groups* and the corresponding study guide titled *Experiencing Small Groups on the Way of Jesus* (along with free video teachings) can serve as practical tools to get groups started.

CHAPTER 4: GATHER IN THE PRESENCE: THE SECOND PRACTICE

[1]See Charles Taylor, *A Secular Age* (Cambridge, MA: Belknap, 2007).

[2]These questions were developed by the people of Beautiful Savior Lutheran Church of Portland, Oregon. Used with permission.

[3]Jim Egli and Dwight Marable, *Small Groups, Big Impact* (St. Charles, IL: ChurchSmart Resources, 2011).

[4]These are adapted from Parker Palmer, *A Hidden Wholeness* (San Francisco: Jossey-Bass, 2004), p. 135.

CHAPTER 5: LEAD COLLABORATIVELY: THE THIRD PRACTICE

[1]Everett Ferguson, *The Church of Christ* (Grand Rapids: Eerdmans, 1996), p. 322.

[2]Gilbert Bilezikian, *Community 101* (Grand Rapids: Zondervan, 1997), p. 97.

[3]Michael Green, *Evangelism in the Early Church* (Grand Rapids: Eerdmans, 1970), p. 25.

[4]Lesslie Newbigin, *The Light Has Come* (Grand Rapids: Eerdmans, 1982), p. 168.

[5]See Gregory A. Boyd, *The Myth of a Christian Nation* (Grand Rapids: Zondervan, 2005), p. 21.

[6]Stanley Hauerwas, *The Peaceable Kingdom* (South Bend, IN: University of Notre Dame Press, 1983), p. 45.

[7]Tom Rath, *StrengthsFinder 2.0* (New York: Gallup Press, 2007).

[8]This is the reason Michael Mack wrote the very helpful guide *The Pocket Guide to Burnout-Free Small Group Leadership* (Houston: TOUCH Publications, 2009).

[9]Jim Egli, "Successful Cell Groups: Critical Factors in Small Group Growth" (PhD diss., Regent University, 2002), p. 92.

[10]John D. Zizioulas, *Communion and Otherness* (New York: Continuum, 2006), pp. 167-68.

CHAPTER 6: BE YOURSELF: THE FOURTH PRACTICE

[1]Ethicist Samuel Wells has served as my guide in identifying the practices of Aristotle's hero.

[2]Samuel Wells, *Improvisation: The Drama of Christian Ethics* (Grand Rapids: Brazos, 2004), p. 44.

[3]John D. Zizioulas, *Communion and Otherness* (New York: Continuum, 2006), p. 89.

[4]Larry Crabb, *The Safest Place on Earth* (Nashville: Word, 1999), p. 11.

CHAPTER 7: HANG OUT: THE FIFTH PRACTICE

[1]Walter Brueggemann, *Disruptive Grace* (Minneapolis: Fortress, 2011), p. 53.

[2]Samuel Wells, *Transforming Fate into Destiny* (Eugene, OR: Cascade Books, 1998), p. 148.

[3]Jean Vanier, *Community and Growth* (New York: Paulist, 1989), p. 47.

[4]Parker Palmer, *A Hidden Wholeness* (San Francisco: Jossey-Bass, 2004), p. 59.

[5]Vanier, *Community and Growth*, p. 14.

[6]Kenneth J. Gergen, *The Relational Being: Beyond Self and Community* (New York: Oxford University Press, 2009), p. 17.

[7]See Christopher J. H. Wright, *Old Testament Ethics for the People of God* (Downers Grove, IL: InterVarsity Press, 2004), pp. 17-20.

[8]For more on this, see Alan J. Roxburgh and M. Scott Boren, *Introducing the Missional Church* (Grand Rapids: Baker Books, 2009), pp. 65-73.

[9]Gary Keller with Jay Papasan, *The One Thing: The Surprisingly Simple Truth Behind Extraordinary Results* (Austin, TX: Bard Press, 2013).

[10]Walter Brueggemann, *Sabbath as Resistance: Saying No to the Culture of Now* (Louisville, KY: Westminster John Knox, 2014), p. 18.

[11]Ibid., p. 10.

CHAPTER 8: MAKE A DIFFERENCE: THE SIXTH PRACTICE

[1]Rodney Stark, *The Rise of Christianity* (New York: Harper Collins, 1996), pp. 73-94.

[2]Eugene H. Peterson, *Eat this Book* (Grand Rapids: Eerdmans, 2006), p. 81.

[3]This *lectio divina* guidance is adapted from David G. Benner, *Opening To God: Lectio Divina and Life as Prayer* (Downers Grove, IL: InterVarsity Press, 2010).

[4]Benner, *Opening to God* (Downers Grove, IL: InterVarsity Press, 2010), p. 74.

[5]Adapted from Jay Pathak and Dave Runyon, *The Art of Neighboring* (Grand Rapids: Baker Books, 2012).

[6]Søren Kierkegaard, *Works of Love,* trans. Howard V. Hong and Edna H. Hong (Princeton, NJ: Princeton University Press, 1995), p. 56.

[7]Ibid., p. 56.

[8]Ibid., p. 36.

[9]Ibid., p. 58.

[10]Andrew Root, *The Relational Pastor* (Downers Grove, IL: InterVarsity Press, 2013), p. 66.

[11]Ibid., p. 67.

[12]Andrew Walls and Cathy Ross, *Mission in the 21st Century* (Maryknoll, NY: Orbis, 2008).

[13]Used with permission.

CHAPTER 9: FIGHT WELL: THE SEVENTH PRACTICE

[1]M. Scott Peck, *The Different Drum* (New York: Simon & Schuster, 1987), p. 90.

[2]Larry Crabb, *The Safest Place on Earth* (Nashville: Word, 1999), p. 50.

[3]Miroslav Volf, *The End of Memory: Remembering Rightly in a Violent World* (Grand Rapids: Eerdmans, 2006), p. 83.

[4]David Augsburger, *Caring Enough to Confront* (Ventura, CA: Regal, 1981), p. 15.

[5]John Howard Yoder, *Body Politics* (Scottdale, PA: Herald, 2001), p. 8.

[6]Roxburgh, "Managing Conflict," p. 43.

[7]Volf, *End of Memory.*

[8]Dietrich Bonhoeffer, *Life Together,* trans. Daniel Bloesch and James Burtness (Minneapolis: Fortress, 1996), p. 90.

[9]Adapted from Rosine Hammett and Loughlan Sofield, *Inside Christian Community* (Le Jacq, 1981), p. 110.

[10]Brian Zahnd, *Unconditional?* (Lake Mary, FL: Charisma House, 2010), p. 41.

[11]These keys were adapted from Daniel Olson's "The Well-Being of Individuals and the Health of the Community" in *The Difficult but Indis-*

pensable Church (Minneapolis: Fortress, 2002), pp. 41-44.

[12]John D. Zizioulas, *Communion and Otherness* (New York: Continuum, 2006), p. 55.

CHAPTER 10: POINT THE WAY TO THE CROSS: THE EIGHTH PRACTICE

[1]This is what Dallas Willard called the VIM model—vision, intention, means—in *Renovation of the Heart* (Colorado Springs, CO: NavPress, 2002), pp. 85-90.

[2]This diagram is adapted from Larry Crabb, *Inside Out* (Colorado Springs, CO: NavPress, 1988), p. 207.

[3]Dietrich Bonhoeffer, *Life Together,* trans. Daniel Bloesch and James Burtness (Minneapolis: Fortress, 1996), p. 44.

[4]Gary Keller with Jay Papasan, *The One Thing* (Austin, TX: Bard, 2012), pp. 57-59.

[5]Bonhoeffer, *Life Together*, p. 82.

Develop a Small Group Ministry in the Way of Jesus

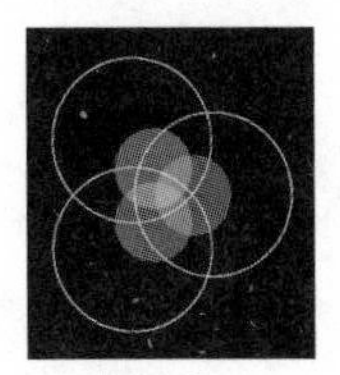

THE CENTER FOR COMMUNITY AND MISSION

Helping churches develop a system and culture that promotes small groups in the way of Jesus.

With more than twenty years of experience consulting with churches, and based on extensive research, we have developed a process that moves a church from its current small group state (or lack thereof) into groups in the way of Jesus. This is more than a program; in fact it's not a program at all. It's a process that helps you discover your unique journey and your unique group model, one that fits your context and your tradition. Check out the consulting and coaching options at the website below.

We also provide training seminars in the following:

- *Leading Small Groups in the Way of Jesus:* A seminar for group leaders
- *Experiencing Small Groups in the Way of Jesus:* A seminar for all group participants that will take groups to the next level
- *Developing a Small Group Ministry in the Way of Jesus:* A seminar on the various systems and structure required to establish a growing small group culture
- *Coaching Small Groups in the Way of Jesus:* Training for those who oversee groups and what is needed for them to serve the groups well
- *Introduction to Missional Community:* A vision-casting seminar on the missional and communal nature of the church

Explore the options at www.mscottboren.com.